FEAR IS A LIAR

HOW TO STOP ANXIOUS THOUGHTS AND EXPERIENCE GOD'S LOVE

DANIEL B LANCASTER

Lightkeeper Books
Nashville, Tennessee

LIGHTKEEPER
BOOKS

LIGHTKEEPER
BOOKS

Fear is a Liar/ Daniel B Lancaster. —1st edition

ISBN 9781086853193

FOR JEFF, LINNEA, AND RHYS

TABLE OF CONTENTS

PREFACE

My prayer is this book will strengthen your walk with God. May you draw closer to Jesus every day and be filled with the Spirit. May you sense deep in your spirit that God loves you and will never let you go.

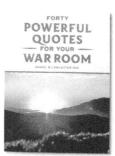  

I have included several bonus gifts that I believe will bless you. The free *Powerful Prayers Bonus Pak* which includes three resources to help you pray powerful prayers:

- 100 Promises Audio Version
- 40 Faith-Building Quotes
- 40 Powerful Prayers.

All are suitable for framing. To download your free *Powerful Prayers Bonus Pak* visit:

go.lightkeeperbooks.com/powerpak

I've also included an excerpt from my bestselling book Fear is a Liar. God has blessed many through this book and I wanted to give you a chance to "try before you buy." Order Fear is a Liar at go.lightkeeperbooks.com/e-fil

If you like the book, please leave a review. Your feedback will help other believers find this book easier and encourage me in my calling to write practical, powerful books to encourage, equip, and empower Christians throughout the world.

Every Blessing,

Daniel B Lancaster
Nashville, Tennessee — March 2022

DISCLAIMER

This book is not intended as a substitute for the medical advice of physicians. The reader should regularly consult a physician regarding their health and particularly about any symptoms that may require a diagnosis or medical attention.

Although the author and publisher have made every effort to ensure the information in this book was correct at the time of publication, the author and publisher do not assume and hereby disclaim any liability to any party for any loss, damage, or disruption caused by errors or omissions, whether such errors or omissions result from negligence, accident, or any other cause.

INTRODUCTION

This is a simple book about how to overcome your fears and experience God's love more deeply.

Doesn't it seem like people used to live simpler, happier lives? Now, many of us are slowly turning into fearful, suspicious people. And fearful, suspicious people are often lonely people. We worry about being rejected by our friends, our loved ones dying, losing our jobs, and failing as parents. We worry about sexual predators, increased crime, the rise in severe weather events, and whether we will have enough money when we retire.

When you try to stop thinking about your fears, they only get stronger. Then, you try to ignore your fears, but that makes them bigger. What's a person to do?

As a missionary, I've faced all kinds of terrifying situations. I've been in earthquakes and hotel fires. I've been trailed by the secret police. Our family moved to a place where soldiers with machine guns guarded every major intersection in the capital city (You can imagine how terrifying it was just driving around). I also know first-hand about the fears that come when ovarian cancer takes your precious wife of thirty years.

I remember a time overseas when all the blood in my body settled in my legs. My wife and I had just learned a mother cobra and her babies decided to live in the flower bed where our children loved to play. A friend discovered the four-foot cobra when it raised its head and swayed back and forth.

Thankfully, he killed the venomous snake and her offspring while we were out of the country renewing our visas. I'll never forget how white my wife's face looked when she heard the news and how I held her arm to steady her.

Our family faced many fearful experiences while we ministered in a foreign land. We had to learn how to deal with our fears or be overwhelmed by them. Sometimes we failed miserably in our fight against fear. Slowly though, we learned the steps in the LOVE Plan and saw more victories than defeats. I believe God will help you do the same.

Jesus said in the last days that fear would increase on the earth. Clearly, people struggle with worry and anxiety today more than ever.

> And there will be signs in sun and moon and stars, and on the earth distress of nations in perplexity because of the roaring of the sea and the waves, people fainting with fear and with foreboding of what is coming on the world. For the powers of the heavens will be shaken.
>
> Luke 21:25–26 (ESV)

In this book, you will learn a biblical plan to overcome whatever fear you may face. God hasn't given you a spirit of fear and wants you to defeat the flaming lying arrows of the evil one.

You will benefit along the way by developing a deeper walk with God and love for other people. You will also discover some good ways to do self-care. This book will teach you how to fill your love tank and not run on "almost empty" any longer.

This book will teach you how to:

- Identify your root fears
- Understand why fears are so powerful
- Learn how Jesus dealt with fear
- Practice a four-step biblical plan to stop fear in its tracks
- Experience deeper love for God, others, and yourself

At the end of this book, my prayer is that you can say:

I prayed to the Lord, and he answered me.
He freed me from all my fears.

Psalm 34:4 (NLT)

Always remember, friend, fear is a liar. I've shared the truth of these principles throughout the world, and they have helped many overcome their fears. I believe God will do the same in your life. As you practice the LOVE Plan, you will hear the Holy Spirit more clearly, and your fears will lose their power over your mind, heart, soul, and spirit.

And it gets even better: You will be able to share these simple truths with your friends and family and see their lives transformed as well. Just imagine the gift you will give your children of knowing how to let perfect love cast out their fears (See 1 John 4:18).

As we journey through this book together, you will learn a new way of living, conquer your fears, and become more like Jesus. God wants that. You want that. I want that. So, let's get started.

In the next chapter, we'll travel back to the first fear recorded in the Bible.

Questions for Reflection

1. Describe a time you tried to ignore a fear, and it got worse.
2. How do you usually handle fear?
3. How has God shown you He is with you when you have been fearful?
4. Write down something that caused a "heart-stopping" moment.
5. Which of your fears are you most eager to tackle first?

1

WHY WE WORRY

Worry often gives a small thing a big shadow.
- SWEDISH PROVERB

Fears are tricky, little devils.

They are like the little weeds in your yard or garden—you hardly give them a thought. But, the longer you wait to remove them, the more weeds they produce. If you wait too long, they choke out the good plants and everything looks ... well... just ugly.

When you feel like the whole world is ugly, it is a sign you have a fear problem. When your relationships feel ugly, it is a sign you have a fear problem. When your God-ordained future seems ugly, it is a sign you have a fear problem.

The first step in overcoming fears is to understand why and where they originally entered the world. That's what we will explore in this chapter. I will show you how Satan first enslaved humanity with fear. It turns out fear and worry have filled people's hearts and minds for an awfully long time.

Along the way, you will discover how the hater tries to manipulate your mind and heart and turn the good from God in your life into evil. You will realize the hater wants you to over analyze everything in your life and paralyze you with fear. This gives Satan even more time to fill your mind with untruths.

Just being aware of his evil schemes will help you walk on the narrow Path of Love instead of wandering on the broad Path of Fear. Understanding why you have fears is an important step to becoming more confident as you fight them.

My prayer is you will once again see the beauty of God brighten every corner of your life. To do that, we will go back to a garden called Eden.

The Narrow Path of Love

Imagine working and playing in the Garden of Eden before Adam and Eve sinned. Everything they did had so much meaning.

Adam and Eve looked forward to the cool of the day. God would come down, and they shared their hearts with Him. He shared His heart with them too. It's easy to imagine what their conversations were like. Love. Love. Love.

Eve shared with God how proud she was of Adam. He was so smart; he had named all the animals! Adam smiled sheepishly and said it was nothing. Eve made him feel ten feet tall.

Adam shared with Eve how lonely life was before she came. Adam thanked God every evening for giving him such an incredible gift. Eve probably blushed and told Adam to stop making such a big deal out of her.

God praised Adam for his heart to be a rock for Eve and someone she could always count on. They noticed a tear in God's eye when He praised Adam for sacrificing for his wife.

God praised Eve for how beautiful she was making everything in the garden and for her creativity. Eve felt so honored and cherished and celebrated.

Oh, the joy to walk on the Path of Love with no fear!

Adam and Eve may have talked with God about having children. They had seen the animals give birth and wondered if humans could too. Or would God make their children as He had made them? Eve looked forward to a happy family that would make the world an even better place.

Adam asked God what had caused him to feel different inside when he climbed too high in a tree.

God explained He had put an emotion in Adam and Eve that told them when they were in danger. He had given them this feeling because He loved them and wanted them to be safe.

Just being close to God filled them with love and confidence. Walking with Him made them feel incredibly strong and wise. God answered every question about their world.

They laughed. They dreamed. They couldn't wait for each day to arrive.

The Broad Path of Fear

But everything changed one day. Adam and Eve stopped walking on the narrow Path of Love. Genesis 3 tells about the painful entry of sin and fear into our world.

> *Now the serpent was more cunning than any beast of the field which the LORD God had made. And he said to the woman, "Has God indeed said, 'You shall not eat of every tree of the garden'?"*
>
> Genesis 3:1 (NKJV)

Satan lures Eve down the Path of Fear by questioning God's command. The Great Manipulator, Satan, takes something good that God has said and makes it sound wrong or petty. He fills her mind with lies.

If you have ever known a self-centered person, you know the drill. Start by getting your target to reconsider a small action or decision. Cause them to doubt their instincts and trust you have their best interests in mind. But it's all a scam. They're luring you into their trap. This is exactly what Satan did in the garden.

Now Eve has started down the Path of Fear, thinking Satan's thoughts, and she doesn't even realize it. Satan has already deceived a third of the angels of heaven into following him. Eve has zero experience dealing with manipulation and deception. There's no way she's going to win.

> *And the woman said to the serpent, "We may eat the fruit of the trees of the garden; but of the fruit*

*of the tree which is in the midst of the garden, God
has said, 'You shall not eat it, nor shall you touch it,
lest you die.' "*

Genesis 3:2–3 (NKJV)

Talking with Satan is never a good idea, but that's exactly
what Eve did. Satan is the Father of Lies and doesn't play
fair. Even though Eve simply tells Satan what God commanded, she is still speaking with the enemy of her soul.
Even Michael, the archangel, knew better than talk to
Satan without God's help (Jude 9).

*Then the serpent said to the woman, "You will not
surely die. For God knows that in the day you eat of
it your eyes will be opened, and you will be like God,
knowing good and evil."*

Genesis 3:4–5 (NKJV)

Now that Eve is thinking the way Satan wants her to, he
openly questions God's goodness. Satan wants Eve to
believe God doesn't have her best interest in mind. God
created Eve as a helpmeet; her deep desire is to work with
Adam to create a beautiful world.

Meanwhile, Satan tells her she is missing out. God is
holding out on her and her husband. She wonders if
God hasn't been telling the whole truth when she and
Adam talked with Him in the cool of the day. Was God
hiding something? Maybe He hasn't been meeting her
needs as well as she thought He was. Satan has fueled
a fire of suspicion in her mind and heart. Can she
even trust God?

*So when the woman saw that the tree was good for food,
that it was pleasant to the eyes, and a tree desirable to*

make one wise, she took of its fruit and ate. She also gave to her husband with her, and he ate.

Genesis 3:6 (NKJV)

Eve relies on her own judgment instead of God's will and God's Word. The fruit looked good. The fruit looked beautiful. The fruit made one wise like God. It's all good.

She takes a bite of the fruit, and nothing happens immediately. So, she gives it to Adam. She probably felt like she had made the best decision in the world, and to show her husband how much she loved him, she shared it with him. Just think how they could help their kids if they were wise like God!

Then the eyes of both of them were opened, and they knew that they were naked; and they sewed fig leaves together and made themselves coverings.

Genesis 3:7 (NKJV)

Enter the first fear: shame. Disobedience opened their eyes and closed their hearts. Adam and Eve saw their nakedness and felt shame. They responded by sewing fig leaves together, trying to hide their shame.

Satan knew the more shame Adam and Eve felt, the more fears they would believe. They soon found that one feeling of unworthiness in the heart can easily create ten fears in the mind.

It's easy to imagine Eve crying and apologizing to Adam for what had happened. Her wrong thinking had created overwhelming suffering for her and her husband. Eve thought she was doing something good.

But everything changed to bad ... extremely bad.

The young couple looked at each other with different eyes. Their feelings of love appeared fake compared to before. Shame and fear were clouding their vision.

The fear emotion they had experienced when climbing too high in a tree had been short-lived. It disappeared after the danger passed. Now they felt fear all the time. For the first time since God created them, Adam and Eve were suspicious of each other.

The Garden of Eden had turned into the Garden of Fear.

And they heard the sound of the LORD God walking in the garden in the cool of the day, and Adam and his wife hid themselves from the presence of the LORD God among the trees of the garden.

Genesis 3:8 (NKJV)

Enter the second fear: guilt. Before Adam and Eve ate the fruit, fear had kept them safe—kept them from danger. But now they felt suspicious and ashamed. Now they hid because they feared God's wrath for their sin.

Terror and trauma replaced the joy of hearing God's footsteps, coming for His evening walk with them.

Adam and Eve had felt peace and security in the Garden of Eden. Now, negative thoughts filled their minds and made them feel hopeless. Their minds raced with bad pictures of the future and regrets from the past.

Eve couldn't stop her mind from thinking of what had happened and what she could do to help them stop feeling bad. She hid from God among the trees with Adam.

Feelings of loneliness, shame, and guilt rose from her heart into her mind, and she felt paralyzed by fear.

*Then the LORD God called to Adam and said to him,
"Where are you?" So he said, "I heard Your voice in the
garden, and I was afraid because I was naked; and I
hid myself."*

Genesis 3:9–10 (NKJV)

If you have ever had a close friendship that ended badly,
you know how Adam felt at this point. Before the fall, he
walked and talked with God. He felt deeply loved and
returned love with no fear. He was free to be creative
and found life fulfilling.

But after the Hater deceived his wife, Adam was overwhelmed with unexpected feelings of shame and guilt.
He felt afraid of God—the Lover of his soul!

We experience these same feelings when we fear. Deep
inside, we say, "I am afraid; I am vulnerable, and I want
to hide myself."

Life can feel hopeless with no plan to overcome constant
fear.

*And He said, "Who told you that you were naked?
Have you eaten from the tree of which I commanded
you that you should not eat?"*

*Then the man said, "The woman whom You gave to be
with me, she gave me of the tree, and I ate."*

Genesis 3:11–12 (NKJV)

Enter the final two fears: blame and rejection.

Adam blames God for what happened, saying, "The
woman whom you gave to be with me." Instead of taking

responsibility for what happened, Adam points an accusing finger at God.

Adam also rejects Eve. He had celebrated her; now, he criticizes her. He had rejoiced in God's gift; now, he rejects her. Why? Hurting people hurt people.

Imagine for a moment the pain of rejection that shot through Eve's heart when she heard those words.

Imagine the fiendish glee in Satan's darkened heart when he saw the tears in Eve's eyes.

Eve wondered where her rock had gone. She felt forsaken. Pictures of feeling distant from Adam the rest of their lives flooded her mind.

> And the LORD God said to the woman, "What is this you have done?" The woman said, "The serpent deceived me, and I ate."
>
> Genesis 3:13 (NKJV)

Adam blamed Eve for what happened. Now Eve blames the serpent.

Her response is short. She probably thinks "less is more." But that approach doesn't work with her Creator. God knows her heart and mind better than she knows them herself.

The Blame Game started in the Garden of Eden and has never stopped. Sadly, blame has just grown more sophisticated through the ages.

- *I know it was wrong, but you made me....*
- *I had a rough childhood, and that's the reason I....*

- *They deceived me, so I had to....*
- *I would have a better life if our leaders would....*

The Blame Game is all about pointing at others, so no one points at you first.

> *So [God] drove out the man; and He placed cherubim at the east of the garden of Eden, and a flaming sword which turned every way, to guard the way to the tree of life.*
>
> *Genesis 3:24 (NKJV)*

Can you imagine Adam and Eve leaving the garden, hiding their faces in shame? Instead of relying on God's love and wisdom, they blamed God, Satan, and each other for what happened.

Clothes made from the furs of innocent animals cover their bodies, but not their overwhelming sense of guilt. God removes them from the garden as an act of love, but they don't see it that way. They feel rejected and cast away.

Adam's loneliness is a thousand times worse than his life before Eve. Eve is still Adam's help meet and wondering how she can help him get rid of these terrible feelings and get them to a better place emotionally.

Both imagine an uncertain future. They no longer feel safe. They feel insecure. Their minds whirl with questions and possible solutions:

- *What will we do the next time we see Satan?*
- *Will God ever talk to us again?*
- *What will our sin and fears do to our children?*

- *Will we ever feel close to each other and God again?*
- *Will our marriage weather this storm?*

In the Garden of Eden, every day was better than the day before, filled with new discoveries and adventures. Now, they believe every day will be worse and filled with difficult problems.

They had depended on God's life-giving wisdom for everything before their sin. Now, they feel mired in negative thinking and dark fears. They began to trust in the creation and not the Creator, and now they are in trouble.

Adam and Eve started walking on the Path of Fear and would continue until the day they died.

Which Path Are You On?

Every person since Adam and Eve starts their journey through life on the Path of Fear. Some people stay on the path forever.

> *We are people of flesh and blood. That is why Jesus became one of us. He died to destroy the devil, who had power over death. But he also died to rescue all of us who live each day in fear of dying.*
>
> *Hebrews 2:14–15 (CEV)*

Living apart from God, we build up a huge amount of guilt, rejection, shame, and blame in our hearts and minds. If we don't deal with these issues, we influence the hearts and minds of our children and others with fear as well.

When you walk the Path of Fear, you believe God is not with you. So you resort to relying on your own thinking, efforts, and plans.

Overcoming your fears is impossible because God is absent, and Satan's work is so strong. You believe everyone is a con.

You forget you are the one choosing what you believe. You are building your own Path of Fear.

When you walk the Path of Love, God is there. His strength, wisdom, and mercy cover you. Walking on the Path of Love strengthens your intimacy with God and makes defeating fears so much easier.

Satan cowers in the presence of Almighty God.

Believers who walk the Path of Love have painful memories, too. They see how their neediness has caused them to drift to the dark side sometimes. The main difference is they repent, return to Jesus, and ask Him to heal their past.

So, how do you walk on the Path of Love?

Some believers teach the answer to the fear problem is to think differently. Think positive thoughts. Don't be so negative. But thinking differently is only half the answer.

Satan has been tempting people with fear since the beginning—for thousands of years. Countless fears. Billions and billions of customers served.

Friend, I care about you enough to tell you the truth.

You don't stand a chance if you are trying to defeat your fears by controlling your negative thoughts. Satan knows too many ways to trip you up. He's been practicing a long time. In comparison, you just started.

If controlling thoughts was the way to defeat fear, Buddhists would be the healthiest, happiest people in the world. But Buddhist countries rank among the poorest and most corrupt. The Buddhist country we lived in for twelve years as missionaries was overcome with fear.

Hmm. Sounds like Satan's rule on the earth—whole countries walking the Path of Fear.

Beautiful people. Bad solution.

Trying to figure out how to control your negative thinking won't solve your fear problem. Some of the smartest people I know struggle with fear the most. Using this approach alone only makes your fears worse.

Why?

Because fear is a head and heart problem.

The answer is a different way of living, not just a different way of thinking. We need a way of living that helps us believe the best is yet to come. Not the other way around.

Questions for Reflection

1. Describe a time you walked the Path of Love without fear.

2. How has Satan made you question God's love for you?

3. Shame, guilt, blame, and rejection are four main fears. How have you struggled with one or more of these?

4. How has relying on your own thinking made things worse?

5. What things will you stop doing to walk on the Path of Fear and start walking on the Path of Love?

2

THE ROOT OF ANXIETY

*Be gentle with yourself, you're doing the best
you can.*

- ANONYMOUS

Have you ever admired a beautiful pearl with all its shimmery color? That beautiful pearl is a result of an oyster fighting against an irritant in its shell. What started out as uncomfortable turned into an accomplishment.

Our fears aren't much different.

It's hard to defeat your fears, but with God's help, it is possible.

It's easy to understand why many people today have a fear problem. Just turn on the news. Have you ever struggled with these common fears?

- I'm afraid of losing my job.
- I'm afraid my kids will be bullied at school.
- I'm afraid my marriage is going to fail.
- I'm afraid I'm messing my kids up with all my problems.

And that's a shortlist. You and I both know we could fill pages and pages with our fears. But let's not go there. Life is hard enough, right?

We want everyone we love to have a healthy, happy life. God has put that desire in our hearts. Jesus said, "I came so that everyone would have life, and have it in its fullest" *(John 10:10b, CEV)*.

In the same passage, however, Jesus warns us that Satan comes to steal, kill, and destroy. Fear is the chief weapon he uses to carry out all three.

The first step in overcoming our fears is exposing the roots of our fears. In this chapter, I will show you the four main fears every person struggles with daily. But before we can overcome these fears, we have to deal with some discomfort along the way.

It may hurt, but in the end, we will shine and hopefully understand our value to God and others.

Learning the Four Root Fears will open your eyes to how Satan is trying to steal your faith, kill your hope, and destroy your love. He wants to keep you silent and to suffer in your fears. He wants to keep you fearful and not confident.

Your fears are hurting you, and your Great Shepherd wants to help you walk beside still waters. Are you ready?

The Four Root Fears Diagram

Let's look at the four greatest fears people face in a way you will never forget. Then, you can share this liberating information with others. May every brother and sister in

Christ be set free from anxious thoughts and experience more love and joy in their lives!

We will draw the Four Root Fears diagram step-by-step together. Then, I'll explain how Satan traps us in each of these core fears. Satan loves unhealthy thinking. He wants to convince you that always having a fear problem is normal. I will show how to break out of his rusty chains.

First, draw a circle. Don't worry if you aren't an artist. Neither am I. It can be our little secret.

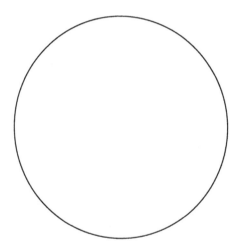

Second, draw a line going up and down the middle. Then, label the top "extrovert" and the bottom "introvert." If you're doing this with a group, help your friends label their circle correctly.

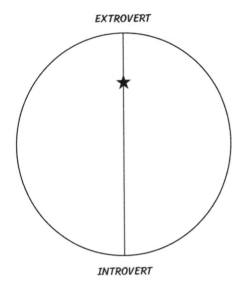

EXTROVERT

INTROVERT

Next, place a mark on the line to show if you are more an extrovert or introvert.

If you are outgoing, have many friends, and love adventure, your mark will be on the top half of the circle.

If you are private, have a few deep friendships, and love safety, your mark will be on the bottom of the circle.

Where are you?

For our example, I will put a mark on the top part of the extrovert side. (That's not me, but I want to show how to make the mark.)

The only rule is you can't place your mark on the center of the line. If you are fifty-fifty, choose one side and draw a mark on the line.

Next, cut the circle in half again with a line going across the middle, making four equal sections. Label the left side "task" and the right side "people."

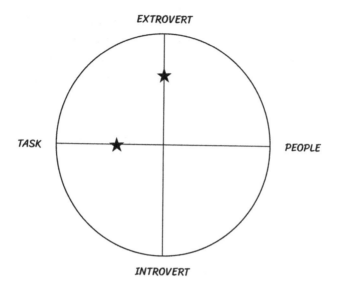

Mark the horizontal line to show how much of a task-oriented person or people-oriented person you are. Again, you can't choose the middle.

The last step is to see where in the circle, the two marks place you.

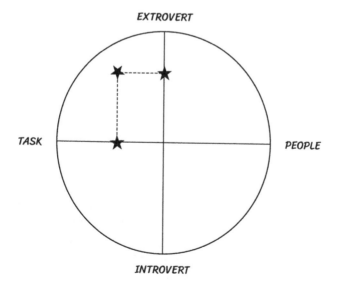

Start at the mark on the task and people line. Draw a line up or down to where it will line up with the mark on the extrovert and introvert line. Then, draw a line across to the mark on the extrovert and introvert line. Where these lines cross is your place on the diagram.

Our Four Biggest Fears

Now we are ready to talk about the Four Root Fears and the two which probably trouble you the most. Everyone struggles with all four fears. Usually, however, two fears give us most of our headaches and heartaches. Knowing which two are your most challenging will give you a head start in defeating Satan's evil schemes to torment you with fear.

Guilt

The first root fear is guilt. Our "example person" falls in this quadrant of the circle. People in this section fear that others will find out the mistakes they have made and not accept them. Feelings of guilt torment them because of the wrongs they've committed.

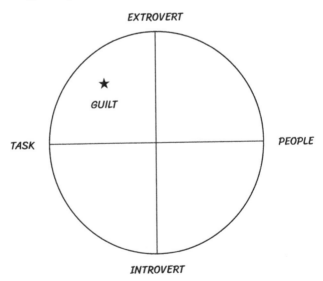

People in the upper left quadrant are often task-oriented extroverts. They want to lead others and achieve tasks, making the world a safer and more secure place for everyone.

Sadly, though, we live in a broken world.

Satan tempts people in this quadrant to make the world better for themselves and worse for everyone else. Most news channels are full of these stories. Many people in this world do evil deeds, and we should look out for them. Jesus said this would only increase as the end of time grew closer.

> But realize this, that in the last days difficult times will come. For men will be lovers of self, lovers of money, boastful, arrogant, revilers, disobedient to parents, ungrateful, unholy, unloving, irreconcilable, malicious gossips, without self-control, brutal, haters of good, treacherous, reckless, conceited, lovers of pleasure rather than lovers of God, holding to a form of godliness, although they have denied its power; Avoid such men as these.
>
> 2 Timothy 3:1–5 (NASB)

If you are in this quadrant, eventually you do something wrong. Even though you have the best intentions and want to make the world a safer place, you still mess up.

So, you fear someone will discover your sin and find you guilty. Satan tells you maybe you will end up on the nightly news like the rest.

People often try to cover their guilt fear by controlling their environment and making others feel guilty for not following the rules the domineering person created.

Another tactic is to make demands on others to deflect the focus from the mistakes and cover up guilt. Unhealthy people in this quadrant never apologize.

Satan loves to chain you in your fears and push your "guilt button" with guilt trips, false guilt, and the guilt of others as well. After a while, Satan just mentions your guilt button, and it goes off with flashing lights and loud sirens in your mind.

He'll do anything to keep you from experiencing life in the present. He wants you stuck in the past—stuck in your mistakes and guilt feelings.

Rejection

The second root fear is rejection. People fear being rejected because of something they say or do or something someone says about them.

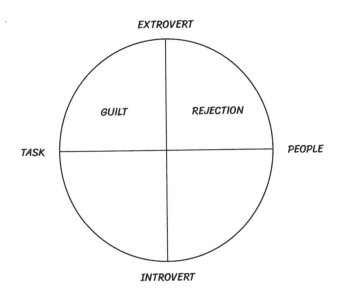

People in the upper right quadrant are people-oriented extroverts. They want to be "out there," helping people make the world a more loving and giving place.

Sadly, though, we live in a broken, dysfunctional world.

Satan tempts people in this quadrant to love themselves by rejecting others. Their mantra is "Reject others before they reject you." Every television drama has a character like this. (Can anyone say, Survivor?)

If you are in this quadrant, you have most likely said something that hurt someone else, probably speaking from your hurt. You wanted the world to be a more loving place, but you contributed to the misery and isolation with a few "choice words."

Or maybe you married someone plagued with fears and hurts from their past. They lash out and reject you for nothing you did at all. After all, hurting people often hurt people.

Personal attacks and painful rejection make us feel needy. With each attack, the Holy Spirit within us mourns.

To cover the rejection fear, you try to perform in ways that will make people happier. You try to say just the right words, so people accept you. You try to do just the right things to appease others. Your attempts to fight the fear of rejection drive you to become a people-pleaser.

> *Fear of man will prove to be a snare, but whoever trusts in the LORD is kept safe.*
>
> *Proverbs 29:25 (NIV)*

And people-pleasing always hurts your relationship with God.

Then Satan whispers in your ear, "You can never please God, you know. He doesn't really love you." In your head, you say it's not true, but in your heart, you start to believe it, and Satan has you trapped ... again.

Shame

The third root fear is shame. People have the fear of guilt because they have done bad things. They have the fear of shame because they believe they are a bad thing.

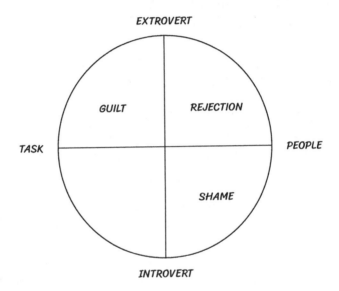

People in the lower right quadrant are people-oriented introverts. They want to work behind the scenes to make sure there is harmony and justice in the world.

Sadly, though, we live in a broken, dysfunctional, cruel world.

People who have endured much shame from their parents or leaders often feel worthless and treat others like they are worthless too. Every movie has a bad guy or gal with a past hurt driving their evil plans.

In our broken world, you discovered it's possible to avoid conflict forever. You wanted the world to be a place of harmony and peace, but you did or said something that caused conflict. So, you feel like you are the bad guy or the naughty gal.

> *I live in disgrace all day long, and my face is covered with shame.*
>
> Psalm 44:15 (NIV)

To cover your shame fear, you decide never to disagree with anyone again. You avoid conflict at all costs. You stuff everything in your emotional suitcase. You are afraid others will discover your shame—your belief that you are a bad person.

All the inner pain finally breaks the dam open one day, and it all spills out. You react way over the top. You totally lose it. You explode. People are surprised by your words and actions. They didn't know you could be the Incredible Hulk.

Then, Satan whispers in your ear, "See, I told you. This proves you really are a bad person. You're a total mess, and now everyone knows it." Satan has you chained like a lonely prisoner of war who no longer remembers the faces of his loved ones and believes he is the one who is bad, not his captors.

Blame

The fourth root fear is blame. People in this category fear others will call them out for poor performance. And they believe poor performance reflects on their character.

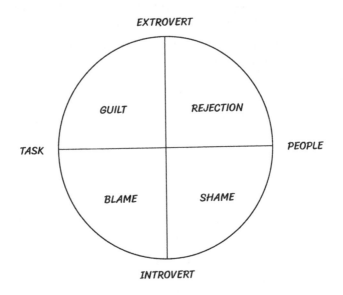

People in the lower left quadrant are task-oriented introverts. They work behind the scenes to make sure everything is high quality.

Sadly, though, we live in a broken, dysfunctional, cruel, and cutthroat world.

Satan tempts some to take shortcuts, use smoke and mirrors, or pretend to be what they are not. The power of deception is obvious in politics. But image worship has seeped into every person, family, community, and nation.

If you are in this quadrant, you have already experienced times in your life when you weren't truthful. You wanted the world to be a true and honest place, but you cut some corners, so you didn't look bad. You compromised your convictions to stay in the game.

I am a joke to people everywhere; when they see me, they shake their heads in scorn.

Psalm 109:25 (NLT)

To cover your fear of blame, you decide to do everything perfectly. Then no one can point a finger at you. No blame can come your way.

Satan delights in pointing out your mistakes. He sneers when you try to arrange your office or home perfectly. He whispers in your ear when you look in the mirror. He paints pictures in your mind of how all your successes will burn to the ground. He tells you if you were a better person, you wouldn't have all these fears.

The more Satan sneers and whispers, the harder you try to be perfect and cover your fear of blame. He's got you right where he wants you.

But keep reading, friend.

God, the Lover of your soul, will show you how to defeat Satan, the enemy of your soul.

Your Two Biggest Fears

I know this chapter has been discouraging.

O.K. It's been downright depressing.

You know your fears are hurting you. They are causing low self-esteem, strained relationships, acting out, and eyes that only see the ugliness in our world instead of the beauty.

Your family and friends love you and want what's best for you. They want you to stop listening to Satan's voice because it's discouraging you. Satan is the Father of Lies. He will just mess up everything ... if you let him.

Dealing with our deepest spiritual problems is always messy. But hang in there. Your hope in God will win the day.

The good news is most people struggle with two of the four fears. When you defeat those two, the other two are much easier to conquer with God's help.

So, let me give you the two fears you should start working on first:

If you are a high extrovert, work on guilt and rejection. Notice when you are controlling and/or being a people-pleaser.

If you are a high introvert, work on blame and shame. Notice when you are struggling with perfectionism and/or avoiding conflict at any cost.

If you are a high task-person, work on guilt and blame. Notice when you are controlling and/or struggling with perfectionism.

If you are a high people-person, work on rejection and shame. Notice when you are people-pleasing and/or trying to avoid conflict at any cost.

If you don't know which one you are, ask a good friend. They have probably known you long enough to know where you land on the circle.

In this chapter, we identified the Four Root Fears believers struggle with on their journey to make the world a better place, enjoy life, and glorify God. You learned how to create a diagram of those fears and how Satan uses our good motivations against us to enslave us.

Then, I gave you the top two fears you should work on first, knowing the other two will be much easier to defeat afterward.

The good news is God promised Adam and Eve in the garden that someday He would crush Satan's head (*Genesis 3:15*). When Jesus died on the cross, He solved our fear problem—forever!

Let's celebrate how God puts the hater down for good in the next chapter.

Questions for Reflection

1. Describe a time God helped you overcome a fear.
2. How does knowing that Satan is behind all fears make you feel?
3. In what ways do you fear people will shame or reject you?
4. If you did the exercises in this chapter, you identified your two main fears. How does that help you in moving forward?
5. What steps will you take this week to work on those fears?

3

DELIVERANCE FROM FEAR

Every moment is a fresh beginning.

- T.S. ELLIOT

Living in a shattered, dysfunctional, unjust, and cutthroat world creates guilt, rejection, shame, and blame: the four horsemen of fear. Satan has sent them throughout the earth to do his evil bidding.

Ever worry about your kids? Satan enjoys using the people we love to throw us on the Path of Fear. It is so easy to fear:

- Car accidents
- Drinking and drugs
- Girlfriends or boyfriends
- Not teaching them everything they need to know
- Not being able to protect them from the world
- Whether they will make good choices or not

When you think about future possibilities, they are usually negative. You try to develop a plan to overcome the future problem (that doesn't exist yet). Then, you feel like the plan might fail, so you try to think up another strategy. Rinse and repeat. Sometimes a hundred times.

Overwhelming feelings of dread fill your heart and mind. You look up and realize you are no longer on the Path of Love.

Satan whispers in your ear, "You'll never get off the Path of Fear. It's impossible."

But fear ... is a liar.

Adam and Eve sinned and brought guilt, shame, rejection, and blame into the world. Like lost sheep, the first couple wandered in deserted places with snakes, wolves, and dangerous cliffs. Fear was everywhere.

Instead of green pastures, they found weeds and thorns. Instead of quiet waters, their hearts felt panic, and their minds silently screamed in terror.

Thankfully, God promised He would send One to crush Satan's head. And at the right time, God did just that.

God sent the Great Shepherd of our souls to guide us back to the Path of Love. Jesus is the only One who can meet your deepest need—love. And He did that on the cross when He defeated sin, death, and every fear: guilt, rejection, shame, and blame.

The Wounded Healer

The prophet Isaiah paints a beautiful portrait of Jesus, our Wounded Healer. As you read this passage, notice how many times Jesus encountered our guilt, rejection, shame, and blame. Truly, He was a man of sorrows.

He was hated and rejected;
his life was filled with sorrow
and terrible suffering.
No one wanted to look at him.

We despised him and said,
"He is a nobody!"
He suffered and endured
great pain for us,
but we thought his suffering
was punishment from God.

He was wounded and crushed
because of our sins;
by taking our punishment,
he made us completely well.

All of us were like sheep
that had wandered off.
We had each gone our own way,
but the LORD gave him
the punishment we deserved.

Isaiah 53:3–6 (CEV)

To overcome your fears, you must put your trust in Jesus's victory over fear on your behalf. If you are a believer, the One who defeated sin and fear lives in you.

Jesus has helped so many people who are like you through the ages. He has given serenity to mothers when their sons left during wartime. He has given peace to fathers during economic downturns. Families have found Him faithful during famines and natural disasters. Children have wept with hope in Him after losing a parent.

Satan tempted all of them to despair. He called them onto the Path of Fear.

But God had a different destiny for His children. Amid their suffering, God promised a better future. Jesus assured this promise on the cross.

Because of Jesus's death and resurrection ...

Guilt is Gone

Jesus took your guilt on the cross when He offered Himself to take the punishment for your sins. Now, you have been declared innocent because you have put your trust in Him.

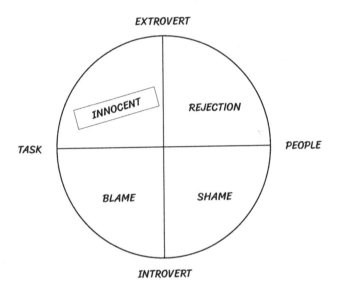

Anytime you do something wrong, confessing your sin to God restores your closeness with Him. Anytime Satan accuses you of wrongdoing, Jesus is the answer. His death on the cross bought your innocence, so don't let Satan torment you with guilt any longer.

In the past, your guilt trips resulted in bad actions. Fears from guilt caused you to be abrasive and controlling. Fears of confessing your guilt hardened your heart and froze your friendships.

You settled for ignoring your hurts, hoping hard work would make them go away.

Those days are gone, child of God! No need to worry about the future. God has it covered. It's time to walk in the cool of the day with your Great Shepherd again. God's grace is so much greater than your guilt.

Rejection is Gone

Jesus bore your rejection on the cross, so you could receive acceptance. You are God's son or daughter now. You are accepted, not rejected.

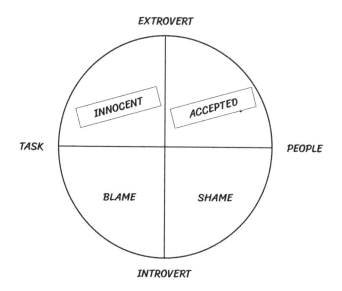

Jesus wants the best for His family, and He doesn't want you tormented by fear. He will guide you in fighting your fears.

His Spirit will empower you and fill your heart with con-fidence—because you are an accepted child of the King!

In the past, you built walls in your heart to protect yourself against rejection. You rejected others before they could reject you. You developed the ability to detect the slightest move toward negative words. You felt vulnerable when you started to get close and raised your shield in protection.

Those days are gone, beloved one! Jesus wants you to focus on the good in your life, not what might go wrong. He wants you to live in the present, enjoy His acceptance, and give it to others. You are accepted by the Great Shepherd ... now and forever.

Shame is Gone

Can you imagine the shame of dying on a cross between two criminals? The righteous and holy Creator of our world, crucified. Jeers. Nails. A crown of thorns. The Highest One became the lowest one.

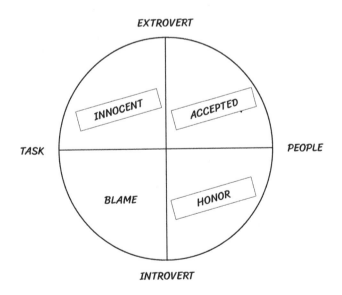

When we were dead in our sins and shame, Jesus died for us, and now we are being transformed into His glory. He took our shame and gave us His honor.

You believed you were flawed and defective. You feared people discovering who you really were. You felt like a nobody and medicated your pain with alcohol, drugs, workaholism, or pornography.

You were afraid to be honest with God and ask for His help. Afraid He would say "no" … afraid He would say, "You aren't worth saving."

But those days are gone, blessed saint of God! The prodigal has come home. Kill the fattened calf. Put on the royal robes. Celebrate in the place of honor. You were dead. But now … you … are … alive!

Honor replaced shame at the cross. In fact, your shame was nailed to the cross.

Jesus is the truth and the way, and you can trust what He says. He says you are a new creation. You are seated with Him in the heavenlies—a place of great honor.

Blame is Gone

Jesus bore our griefs and carried our sorrows on the cross. Our sins caused us to miss the mark of living rightly for God. Yet He took the blame for our sin, though He never did anything wrong.

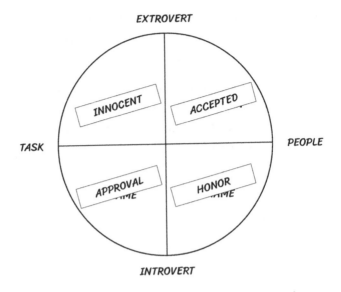

Take your hardest day with the heaviest burden, multiply it a billion times, and you only begin to understand what it meant for Jesus to shoulder your blame and mine. What incredible strength!

Somehow, every person remembers the Garden of Eden—a beautiful place of peace and security. In the past, you frantically tried to recapture paradise by being perfect. You depended on your strength—your mind, talents, and abilities. But your efforts proved no match to fear. So many days you spent crumpled on the floor in tears, crying out to God for help.

But those days are gone, anointed child of God! You need not fear blame any longer. You can stop trying to be perfect. Instead, depend on the strength of the perfect One living in you.

Jesus wants you to know you are no longer under condemnation. You aren't to blame.

It's time to enjoy being smart, talented, creative, and a good problem-solver again. You have God's everlasting seal of approval.

Who Do You Follow?

Jesus crushed our fears on the cross. He bore all the guilt, rejection, shame, and blame of every person who has lived, is living, and will live. Hallelujah! What a Savior!

Most people believe God could never understand their circumstances since Adam and Eve left the garden. He is too perfect. Too holy. Too wise. How could He understand the fears ruling my life right now?

But He does understand. He came and lived among us.

He faced Satan like we face Satan, and He won!

He faced death like we face death, and He won!

He faced fear like we face fear, and He won!

Jesus doesn't lose. And He lives in you. So, you won't lose either.

Fear was originally a gift on the Path of Love to protect us. God made people with the ability to fear when they were in danger. Without the emotion of fear, people would constantly be in danger of hurting themselves.

However, Satan deceived Eve, using her good desires to trick her. As Satan's plan succeeded to hurt the ones God loved most, sorrow came into the world.

Sin changed Adam and Eve's minds and hearts. Instead of sensing God's love, they now felt guilt, rejection, shame, and blame. God's love for them never stopped, though. They had altered the course of all creation, but God still cherished them. God still wanted to walk with them in the cool of the day.

Since then, people have tried many solutions to stop their anxious thoughts. But sin has planted the four main fears in the center of the human heart. No amount of thinking or trying could remove them. You've tried. I've tried. Everybody has tried ... and failed.

Until Jesus came.

Only God's Son could pay the price, offer the perfect sacrifice, and die for the sins of humanity. His victory over sin includes defeating the four fears too.

So, it all comes down to this:

- Satan walks the broad Path of Fear.
- Jesus walks the narrow Path of Love.
- Which path are you walking on?

Many believers know the spiritual truths of the last few chapters, but they don't have a practical way to apply them—a way to walk them out. Sadly, they travel on the Path of Fear more often than the Path of Love.

What you and I need is a simple plan that will help us consistently walk with Jesus on the Path of Love. We need a powerful plan that keeps us from drifting over to the Path of Fear.

In the next chapter, you will learn how to use the LOVE Plan—a simple, biblical way of defeating fears anytime, anywhere.

Are you ready to stop your anxious thoughts and feel the love of God again? Let's do this.

Questions for Reflection

1. What's holding you back from trusting God with your loved ones?

2. How has Jesus given you peace about your family members in the past?

3. How is your guilt holding you back from the embrace of our loving Savior's arms?

4. Describe a time when you experienced God's forgiveness in the past.

5. What do you need to confess to our Lord today?

4

HOW TO STOP ANXIOUS THOUGHTS

*Just when the caterpillar thought the world was
ending, he turned into a butterfly.*

- ANONYMOUS

Now things get exciting. I am praying the next few
chapters completely transform your life. By God's
grace, I believe they will.

You understand where fear started, the four core fears,
and how Jesus has conquered each one. You have identified
the two core fears that beat you down the most.

Now, I will share a simple, powerful plan to give you a
way to fight back. And win.

The LOVE Plan has four steps, and they are easy to
remember:

L is for listen

O is for observe

V is for value

E is for expect

Using this four-step plan with God's help, you can defeat your fears and return to the Path of Love. Your eyes will open to the wonder of God's creation, and your faith will grow as you walk with Him.

Your relationships with God, family, and friends will improve significantly. You will learn how to love yourself the way God loves you too.

Let's look at each step of the plan and start crushing your fears.

Listen

The first step in the LOVE Plan is to listen. If you're hearing the Lord's voice, He will direct you to stay on the Path of Love. When you feel anxious or worried, try to decide whose voice is creating the fear. Why? Because the truth sets us free.

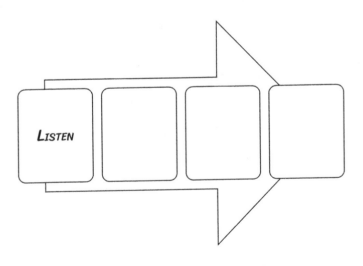

My sheep hear My voice, I know them, and they follow Me.

John 10:27 (HCSB)

If the voice is your own, you may be walking on the Path of Love or the Path of Fear.

If the fear is in the present—like a bear chasing you—it's your voice on the Path of Love. God put this emotion in you to protect you. Run!

If the fear is in the past or the future—like worrying your friend will be in a car wreck next month—it's your voice on the Path of Fear. You have not renewed your mind about that thought with the Word of God.

If you sense fear because you have disobeyed one of God's commands, repent and God will restore your closeness to Him. When we sin, fear is like the warning light on a car. We can't ignore the light—we need to stop and fix the problem. If you are feeling convicted, don't ignore it; God wants you to turn from your sin and return to the Path of Love.

If the voice is Satan's, the tempter is trying to pull you over to walk on the Path of Fear. The fear will usually have something to do with losing your possessions, someone you love, or your reputation.

As you already know, Satan often disguises his voice by using the voice of someone or something else.

Satan whispers something your mom said to you in the past to create fear and take the wind out of your sails.

Satan mimics your dad's warning about something in the future to stoke the fire of fear within you.

Satan speaks through the nightly news to say, "Look at all the problems in the world. Where is God?"

Satan speaks through blog posts to say, "Look how the church in America is failing. Why would anyone want to follow Christ?"

Satan repeats something your friend said in anger and convinces you they really meant it.

Finally, the voice may be someone in your life who hurt you because they were walking on the Path of Fear. It's not Satan's voice, but the voice of a struggling, fellow traveler who wounded you or maybe an evil person who maimed you.

Sometimes, it can be difficult to figure out where the voice is coming from—especially if you were abused as a child at home or school.

You don't have to nail the voice down exactly. But a general rule of thumb is this: any voice that tries to put fear in you is not from God. Over time, you'll find the Holy Spirit will give you deeper understanding and healing. This doesn't happen overnight but determining where the voice is coming from if you can is worth it.

Like every good shepherd, Jesus wants his followers to be healthy and feel safe. It blesses Jesus when He sees you stop, listen, and try to detect whose voice is causing the fear in your mind and heart. The more you hear His voice, the more love you will feel. And the more you know His voice, the easier it is to recognize when fear is trying to creep in.

Once you have identified the voice, the next step is to OBSERVE.

Observe

The first step of the LOVE Plan is to LISTEN and find the source of your fear. In the second step, you step back and OBSERVE what the fear is doing in your body, mind, and emotions.

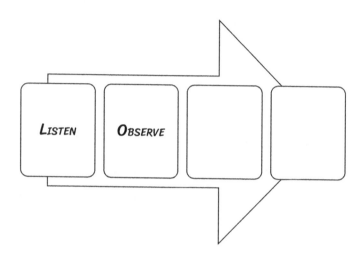

We don't think about it often, but God is always looking at us. Jesus, as the Great Shepherd of your soul, constantly watches over you. He sees you when you are talking with friends. He sees you when you are driving to work or playing with your children.

> But the LORD watches over those who fear him, those who rely on his unfailing love.
>
> Psalm 33:18 (NLT)

Unlike an earthly shepherd, though, Jesus also sees your mind and heart. To put it another way, Jesus observes everything you do, say, feel, and believe.

In this step, we ask Jesus to tell us what He is observing about our struggle with fear. Hearing His observations gives our mind a chance to rest from over-analyzing everything.

One of Satan's main tricks is to keep you mulling over your fears until you are so tired you will believe anything.

What does the Good Shepherd see in your body?

- Is your heart beating faster?
- How is your breathing?
- Is your stomach in knots?
- Do you have a headache?

What does the Good Shepherd see in your mind?

- Are you so stressed you can't focus?
- Is your mind running a million miles an hour?
- Do you feel like your mind is going to explode?
- Are you struggling with forgetfulness?

What does the Good Shepherd see in your heart?

- Is the fear making you feel sad, mad, or bad?
- How strong are your emotions right now?
- What circumstances have caused this emotion in the past?
- On a scale from 1 to 10, how hopeless is this fear making you feel?

Jesus knows we live in a shattered, dysfunctional, unjust, and cutthroat world because of Adam and Eve's sin. If we believe the fears and voices from this world don't affect us, we are living in denial. Fear affects our heart, mind, and body, and it's important to recognize this as we walk out the LOVE Plan.

Looking into the eyes of your Savior and seeing what He sees in you helps you judge the voice you are listening to and prepares you for the next step: VALUE.

Value

Satan wants to hinder the plans God has prepared for your life. He wants to chain you to the Path of Fear.

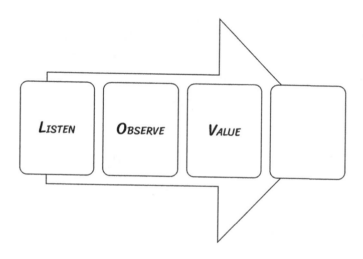

The hater knows when you feel vulnerable and needy, he can trap you in worry and anxiety. And the quickest way to make you feel weak, vulnerable, and needy is to fill your mind and heart with fear.

But Jesus wants you to know the truth, so you can live fear-free. And here's the truth.

Most fears are false positives.

Unless you are in physical or mental danger and should flee, fears are almost never true. When you shine the light of God's love on them, they disappear like the mirages they really are.

Our heart is like a love tank. When that tank is full, we feel confident—able to face whatever may come our way. When our love tank is edging toward empty, we fear rejection and struggle to get out of bed.

In the third step, you VALUE yourself the way Jesus values you. This fills your love tank and gives you every spiritual blessing to overcome your darkest fears. And the more you experience God's acceptance, honor, and approval, the less fear will trouble you.

> *Just as the Father has loved Me, I have also loved you; abide in My love.*
>
> *John 15:9 (NASB)*

We don't take thoughts captive by fighting them with our mental strength. We take thoughts captive by letting God's love settle over our hearts. Then, our minds follow.

Fears will come. They are Satan's favorite weapon against God's children. With the VALUE Step, you make sure your love tank is full. There is nothing Satan hates worse than God's love because it crushed his head forever on the cross.

And remember, God promised that perfect love casts out fear (1 John 4:18). When we are filled up with God's love, fear doesn't stand a chance!

Start taking your fears captive today by relying on God's love to flood your heart, not on your ability to think positively. Thinking positively is no problem when you feel loved.

As you receive God's love and expose most fears as the posers they are, you are ready for the next step: EXPECT.

Expect

Have you ever caught yourself dreaming about how wonderful a fear-free life would be? The dark clouds of fears about your kids, health, marriage, or work no longer hanging over your head ....

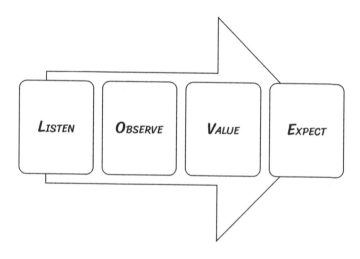

Ever noticed God isn't in the picture when you fear? He's nowhere to be found. Your fear convinces you this is a problem you must solve yourself with your own strength, your own thinking, and your own courage.

The quickest way to jump on the Path of Fear is to believe you can handle everything in your life. It makes you a sitting sheep.

Well, at least you will be able to sing, "I did it my way."

But it doesn't exactly work that way, does it? Fear has punched a hole in your love tank, and you are going down fast. Satan knows the only way to drain your tank is to keep you focused on yourself and not exercising faith in God.

The EXPECT Step is to believe God will be with you in every circumstance you face. Always. Forever.

> Faith shows the reality of what we hope for; it is the evidence of things we cannot see.
>
> Hebrews 11:1 (NLT)

When fear paints a scary picture in your mind, automatically put God in the picture. Close to despair? God is beside you. An unexpected storm? God is with you. The darkest night of your soul? He's close to the brokenhearted.

You are not alone. You will never be alone. You can expect God always to be close, guiding you every step of the way. He is the Good Shepherd, and you can expect He will never leave you behind.

▼ ▼ ▼ ▼ ▼

The LOVE Plan is a simple, yet powerful way to conquer your fears. The more you practice the four steps, the more skilled you will become at crushing your fears.

The first two steps in the LOVE Plan involve your mind: LISTEN and OBSERVE.

The last two steps concern your heart: VALUE and EXPECT.

An effective strategy for defeating fear must address both the mind and heart.

In the next chapter, we will learn how to hear God's voice better. Let him who has ears hear.

Questions for Reflection

1. Record your thoughts about the idea of moving forward with the LOVE plan.

2. How is God telling or showing you He loves you?

3. How do you feel knowing the Good Shepherd sees all that you are going through?

4. Write down three ways you will take your fears captive.

5. Write a prayer to God, thanking Him for always being with you no matter what you are facing.

5

I HEAR HIS VOICE

In the end, just three things matter:
How well we have lived.
How well we have loved.
How well we have learned to let go.

- JACK KORNFIELD

Many people struggle to hear God's voice in this chaotic world. Discerning God's voice is especially difficult if the enemy has deceived you before. You thought you were listening to God's voice, but Satan turned himself into an angel of light and tricked you.

Satan left you wounded and bleeding. Now you have doubts.

I've been there. It makes it difficult to trust God. It makes it difficult to trust your decisions. Your confused heart battles all kinds of fears.

The good news is you now have a plan to help you defeat fear in any circumstance. You have an easy-to-remember plan to keep you on the Path of Love—far from the Path of Fear.

Your life can be green pastures, still waters, and a table set before your enemies (Psalm 23). That is the life God promises His children.

In this chapter, we will look at four keys to hearing God's voice better.

All That Glitters

Satan's full-time job is to convince you to listen to his voice and not God's (Remember, this is exactly what he did with Adam and Eve in the garden). He knows you will grow as a believer the more you follow God's voice. He knows you will start thinking the way God thinks—positively—and that will ruin the evil one's negative plan.

Satan wants you to follow him on the Path of Fear. And he has perfected many techniques to win you over. Usually, he takes a basic need we have and magnifies it to tempt us. Let's look at a few examples.

We need money. Without money, we can't buy food, pay for our home, or keep the lights on. God has promised He would meet all our needs. Money isn't bad, but loving money is.

Then Satan comes and says, "Look at how good God is taking care of that family over there. Wonder why He isn't meeting your needs like that?"

We take our eyes off the blessings God has given us and focus on the blessings He has given others. Then, we grow suspicious and fear God might take away what we have because He doesn't really care about us.

Satan's caught us—hook, line, and sinker.

Here's another example: we think we need a sense of control in our lives—a sense of personal power. We don't want to be bound against our wills. We want the freedom to create and carry out whatever the Lord has given us to do. Believers know that surrendering to the Holy Spirit fills them with God's power.

But Satan comes and says, "Those people are trying to control you and take credit for what you have done. You need to stand up for your rights. You need to learn how to control them instead. The more power you exert, the more people will respect you. You don't want to be a slave to them, do you?"

The teeth of Satan's trap crush our hearts and maim us before we even know it.

He tried the same line with Jesus:

> *Again, the devil took Him to a very high mountain and showed Him all the kingdoms of the world and their glory; and he said to Him, "All these things I will give You, if You fall down and worship me."*
>
> *Matthew 4:8–9 (NASB)*

Remember, Jesus knows how you feel when Satan tempts you with glitter and fool's gold.

At this point, you may be thinking, "I haven't fallen for those traps. I'm good." I hope you haven't, but let's dig a little deeper.

People who listen to the deceiver's voice often believe the following:

- The more money we have, the safer our future will be.

- The more intimacy we have, the safer our marriage will be.
- The more popular I am on social media, the better people will think of me.
- The more beautiful or handsome I am, the better mate I will attract.

The list is endless. Just know that whenever you start saying, "The more..." you are no longer on the Path of Love. You are walking the Path of Fear or have fallen into a muddy ditch somewhere in between.

Love doesn't say, "The more...."

Satan tries to get you to feel dissatisfied with your life, to want what you don't have, and to worry about how you'll get it. (Sound familiar? That's what he pulled with Eve in the garden). He tells you that your life won't be okay unless something changes.

We call this game the "More Game" at our house. I wish I could say we have never played it, but we have. Turning the volume down on commercials helps sometimes. Ministering in a third-world country for twelve years made the biggest difference. It's hard to want more when you live among starving people who send their children to beg for the family's only meal of the day.

We only fall for the "More Game" when our love tanks are on empty. Like hazard lights on the highway warning of trouble, craving more and more is a sign of danger—spiritual danger.

"Bigger is Better" is another game Satan plays with us. It's the same old trick. I've noticed the trouble with getting bigger possessions is they take more money, time, and work to protect.

Satan tempts you to focus on feeling good about yourself by buying a bigger home. Then, he tempts the thief to break into your bigger home because you have something the thief wants. It's a win-win for Satan and a lose-lose for you.

Satan says, "Just do it." But everything that glitters isn't gold, friend. Don't fall for Satan's deception and lies.

Jesus says, "Follow Me, and I will meet all your needs— now and forever."

Stop the Stampede

When you learn how to hear God's voice better, you will realize many voices you have been hearing are those of your family and friends, past and present. They mean well, but they don't always give the best advice about overcoming fear.

The problem with listening to your family and friends is they have fears too. They may be too happy to give their opinion about what's wrong with you.

But if their counsel isn't based on the voice of the Great Shepherd, it's like a flock of sheep telling one another the best path and how to avoid danger. Usually, the whole flock bolts in fear and stampedes over the same cliff. And it's not a pretty sight.

Instead of enjoying the still waters of the Great Shepherd, you get stuck in the muddy water with the frightened herd. Instead of the green pastures God has promised, you wander in deserted wastelands full of ravenous wolves ready for their next meal.

Your friends may even tell you that having fears is just normal and not to worry about them. Don't all parents worry about their kids? Doesn't everyone worry about their job?

But worry is like cancer to your soul. Would you tell someone with cancer not to seek treatment? You need to crush your fears, friend. And you can by using the LOVE Plan.

When you listen to the Great Shepherd, you experience unending love, instead of unending fear. That's the life I want to live. How about you?

So, consider not hanging out with friends who always see dark clouds in the future. Be careful around family members who encourage you to play the "bigger" and "better" games to preserve your image.

Know that when you see yourself angry, controlling, rejecting, shaming, and blaming, these are like your car indicator lights. If the indicator light is on, it means you are listening to the wrong voice.

If you listen to God's voice, you will say "no" to your flesh— "no" to the "bigger" and "better." God will comfort your heart and remind you that most of your fears are frauds.

Worry can easily become a bad habit. Now is the time to lean into Jesus and make the LOVE Plan your habit.

> *You will keep the mind that is dependent on You in perfect peace, for it is trusting in You.*
>
> *Isaiah 26:3 (HCSB)*

So, give up overthinking your life. Listen to God first instead of trying to come up with your plan. Satan wants to keep you in your negative thought patterns. He wants to plow deep, ragged rows of negativity in your mind. He'll even get you to be negative about being negative to sidetrack you from defeating your fears.

God, on the other hand, wants to create a beautiful Garden of Eden in your mind and heart with the fruit of the Spirit. After asking Jesus to save you, listen to the sweet voice of truth from the lover of your soul, and He will create a fruitful, peaceful garden in your heart and mind that is more beautiful than you can imagine.

More Slippery Customers

Defeating your fears is important because they are the main obstacles to the self-confidence and love God wants you to enjoy every day. Solve this problem, and living water will flood out of your inner being.

Satan loves to take times in your past when you felt insecure and project them into the future. He wants you to believe they will happen again. He plays those old movies on the screen of your mind, and they seem so real.

But always remember ... fear is a liar.

Whenever you question your abilities and self-worth, ask yourself whose voice you are listening to. Jesus wants you to hear His voice over the thundering crowd. He doesn't want your feelings of not being good enough to cripple you.

[Satan] was a murderer from the beginning, not holding to the truth, for there is no truth in him. When he lies,

he speaks his native language, for he is a liar and the father of lies.

John 8:44 (NIV)

It may seem like you are listening to your fourth-grade teacher who said you would never amount to anything in front of the class. But she was merely the mouthpiece for the accuser of your soul.

Satan brings up old memories to make us feel vulnerable. And when we feel vulnerable and unsafe, we fear. Sadly, the more we fear, the more vulnerable and unsafe we feel. It is a vicious, mind-numbing cycle.

Does it seem like the world used to be a happier place? Do you feel there's nothing you can do to change how bad people are becoming? Stop and ask yourself, "Who am I listening to right now?"

Satan wants you to stay glued to the television screen, watching every bad event happening in the world. He whispers in your ear how life used to be so much easier for people.

The accuser wants to convince you that you are powerless to produce any change ... that no matter what, you are doomed to a life with no success, no joy, and no hope.

But, he's a con artist.

Let me say that again. He's...a...con...artist!

The Creator of everything bright and beautiful lives in you and millions of believers around the world. God's kingdom is coming, and His will is being done throughout the earth.

In His mighty power, God is always turning what the enemy meant for evil into good. You just don't hear much of that on the news, do you?

And Satan wants it that way.

Bad news is good news for the news media. That's how they get ratings to sell advertising and build their empire. I think we both know it isn't their kingdom, though. Too many times they are merely a production studio for the deceiver.

Jesus wants you to see through the ploy of the voices on your screen. They are peddling sensationalism, terror, and trouble to capture your attention and torment you with worry and fear. God gave you the fear emotion to protect you, but Satan is using it to enslave you.

Ask God for Help

Did you know God wants you to hear His voice? He spoke through the Old Testament prophets, so His people could hear Him. Later, He sent His Son into the world, so we could hear Him speak in a human voice.

Jesus spoke God's truths and promised to leave His peace with us. Instead of being relentlessly plagued by fear, we can experience God's peace through the presence of the Holy Spirit. The more you strengthen your connection with God's Spirit, the stronger you will be when you confront your fears.

On the other hand, Satan tempts us to think of all the bad in our past. The deceiver wants you to forget all the times the Spirit of God carried you, loved you, and healed you.

Satan wants you to forget all the walks you had with God in the cool of the day. Satan wants you to focus on fear and forget the loving people God has put in your life. He wants you to feel alone and believe no one can help you. The devil just doesn't play fair, does he?

While Satan tries to entangle us in his web of worry, I don't think the One with all authority and power who defeated Satan and death worries about anything! What do you think? No way! Jesus was so full of God's love that fear had no hold on Him, and He wants to help us do the same.

Now here's the good news: God wants you to ask Him for help with your fears. He has sent the Holy Spirit to help you.

The question is ... will you let Him?

- Ask the Holy Spirit to show you what voice you are listening to and why.
- Ask the Holy Spirit to give you "ears to hear" what God is saying to you.
- Ask the Holy Spirit to strengthen your heart and renew your mind against fears.
- Ask the Holy Spirit to heal the trauma in your life and put you back on the Path of Love.

And then......stop......and......listen.

The Holy Spirit will cut through Satan's smoke and mirrors and show you why you are in a fog of fear. God will show you how your past is keeping you from being fearless in the present. He will convict you of old ways of thinking that must go.

When the Spirit of truth comes, He will guide you into all the truth. For He will not speak on His own, but

He will speak whatever He hears. He will also declare to you what is to come.

John 16:13 (HCSB)

If you follow the LOVE Plan, you can turn what Satan has meant for evil into the good God intended all along. Your fears can be a warning light to stop and listen and deepen your dependence on God.

The more you listen to God's Word, the better you will recognize Satan's tricks. And the more you listen to God's voice, the more you will feel loved. And the more loved you feel by God, the more fear will be driven out of your life.

LISTEN is the first step of the LOVE Plan because it deepens your bond with God, and that is the starting place for crushing your fears.

In the next chapter, I'll show you how the OBSERVE Step of the plan quickly calms your heart and mind.

Questions for Reflection

1. Describe a time when you asked God for direction or wisdom, and He showed you what to do.

2. Write down a time when you received an unexpected blessing from God (money, encouragement from someone, material possessions, etc.).

3. What steps will you take to choose not to worry? How will you encourage others not to worry?

4. How has God used bad things in your life for good?

5. Spend some extra time today in prayer, asking the Holy Spirit to allow you to hear, strengthen you, and heal your hurts.

6

HE CARES FOR ME

There are far, far better things ahead than anything we leave behind.

- C.S. LEWIS

Right now, Jesus is painting the mosaic of your life in living color. Every bristle of His brush is creating and shaping the landscape and your surroundings. His careful gaze is making sure everything is done with the utmost care.

A little more color here. A little less there. His sculpting knife tones down the excess. Shapes and movement form unique impressions on the canvas.

Blues. Greens. Reds. Yellows. All mixed perfectly into His masterpiece—you.

But many times, we don't see our lives that way. Fears make us feel like we are living in a black and white horror film or a foreign film with bad subtitles. It's easy to lose perspective, isn't it?

Thankfully, God has given us everything we need to overcome our fears. God constantly works in us to make us more like His Son.

The OBSERVE Step of the LOVE Plan helps you become more objective about the fears you face. Looking at your fears the way Jesus looks at them brings inner peace. Seeing how your body is reacting to fears reduces them into more manageable foes.

In my experience, this step alone cuts the power of fear in half. Fears snivel and shrivel under the powerful gaze of King Jesus.

Let's explore some practical ways to activate the OBSERVE Step and discover why it is so effective against fears.

My Father's Eyes

Life has a way of beating us down and leaving us for dead in the rubble of low self-esteem. Because we live in a broken world, we run into negative experiences every day. Satan wants to hang those negative experiences in your heart as huge game trophies to prove God doesn't care for you.

You notice you don't enjoy hanging out with friends as much as you used to. You're afraid of what they might say or do. It's just easier to stay home alone than take a chance on getting hurt.

People compliment you, but you shrug it off. You fear they are trying to manipulate you by masking secret requests with kind words and asking for more than you can give. You tell yourself, "They don't really mean what they said. They were just being nice."

You give others the benefit of the doubt. You are fair to them. But you aren't fair with yourself. When hard times come, you believe you actually deserve them. You would never treat someone else badly, but you routinely criticize and make fun of yourself … secretly … silently.

And maybe you tried to say positive affirmations to yourself a thousand times to improve your self-image. But it didn't work. Somewhere deep down, you felt like even having to say positive affirmations only further proved how defective you were.

The answer you're seeking lies in the OBSERVE Step. You need to slow down and practice the spiritual exercise of contemplation.

Simply put, you seek the face of God in everything you encounter. You look for His hand moving in every part of your life.

You find God during prayer, but also when you are playing with your children. You feel God during worship, but also in projects with deadlines at work. You see God touching, healing, and laughing and singing among the poor and the powerful. When you look, God is everywhere.

Ever ride a fast roller coaster? It's a scary experience.

Running through life too fast? It's also a scary experience.

I know you have a lot you want to accomplish. You want to be successful. You want to be an awesome parent. You want to be an amazing best friend.

But please slow down and watch for Jesus in everything. "Look full in His wonderful face," as the old song says. "And the things of earth will grow strangely dim."

Shut your eyes and look into the eyes of Jesus. Is He teary-eyed about you today? Does He have a look of pride because of a goal you achieved? Does He look concerned?

After you spend time pondering the glory and love of the Lord, turn your attention to your fears.

When going into battle, a wise commander learns as much about his enemy as possible. Observing your fears gives you invaluable military intelligence. The battleground is your heart and mind, so take time to discover all you can about yourself.

Keep a journal as you study your fears. Record all the details you can remember about the fear. Rate how intense the fear was and any patterns you noticed leading up to its assault. Be honest with yourself. The journal is for you and God alone.

The greatest benefit of spiritual contemplation is it helps you embrace your perfect imperfections. Look up into the face of Jesus. Then look down at your fears. Finally, write about what God is showing you in your journal. This process will help you understand and accept the masterpiece God is creating in you.

All your imperfections are the unique and perfect strokes of God Almighty. What you think are flaws or rough edges are His design. Yes, it's true. God loves your nose and your ears and your lips and ... well, you get the idea.

Too many people try to Photoshop their lives into a perfect image. Can anyone say, "social media?" A quick question, though. Why go for a manufactured copy when you can have the priceless masterpiece fashioned by your Creator?

Jesus was fully God and perfect. Jesus was also fully man with the imperfections of these earthly bodies. Embracing your perfect imperfections draws you closer to Him. It's hard to imagine Jesus "correcting" a photo of Himself before He posted it on Facebook, isn't it?

So be the transparent and real person God made you to be. Nothing more. Nothing less. Live like that, and you won't have anything to hide or fear.

Little Sparrow

When we visited the markets in Southeast Asia, you would often see an old woman with a cage of small birds. In Buddhism, you receive good karma if you set a bird free. So, people would give her their pocket change to set a bird free.

On one occasion, I gave the taunt-faced woman a few dollars—enough money to release all her birds. She smiled and opened the cage. The birds quickly flew out the cage into the sky, making wide circles. I don't believe in karma, but it felt good to see them free.

After we finished shopping, we returned the same route and saw the old woman again. She had another cage of birds. She begged for money as she had before with a grin showing her yellow or missing teeth.

Turns out she had caught the birds and trained them to return to the cage after she released them. Satan has trained your fears to do the same. Observing your fears brings his deceit into the light instead of keeping them in the dark.

When you practice contemplation, you may discover all your busy activities have merely been an attempt to cover the fact you don't accept yourself.

God may show you how you have been punishing yourself. Your self-talk is full of guilt, loneliness, and insecurity. You're convinced you are unattractive and lazy. You wonder how anyone would love you if they knew what you were really like.

I believe the Spirit has one comment about that mentality: Satan is already a hater; you don't need to be one too.

This is a stage you will go through as you learn to observe your fears. It's normal. Don't let it surprise you.

Spiritual contemplation enables you to move past the places of denial in your life into reality and acceptance.

So often, we ignore how we feel about our relationships and job. We look past problems with our health and our children. We don't want to tell the emperor he has no clothes—much less ourselves.

But let's get real.

If you saw a friend struggling with fear, you would be sad to see how the fear affected their body. Maybe they would be sweating or breathing quickly. Or their eyes filled with terror.

Whatever sign of fear you noticed, your heart would reach out to your friend and want to help them. And that's how God the Father responds when He sees you struggling with fear: He won't leave you there.

God has always loved you. He loves you now. He will always love you. If Satan has convinced you to not love yourself, God won't stand for it.

The Spirit of God will give you the power to conquer your fears—even though you have been defeated many times before. The more you practice the OBSERVE Step, the more Satan's lies will repulse you. His lies will smell like rotting roadkill on a hot August afternoon.

The Spirit has never been afraid. He is full of confidence and creativity. He has given you the power you need to live for Him in this life. Lean into Him.

The Good Shepherd will remind you of Scripture promises about His care. He will intercede for you before the Father, asking for a breakthrough.

His eye is on the sparrow. Note how He takes care of the sparrows. Watch how He takes care of you too.

> *Indeed, the very hairs of your head are all numbered. Do not fear; you are more valuable than many sparrows.*
>
> *Luke 12:7 (NASB)*

Jesus sees the same responses to fear you are seeing, and His gaze is full of approval and acceptance. No need to feel ashamed, child of God. Seeing events the way Jesus sees them makes you more like Him.

Little sparrow, let Jesus take you under the shadow of His wings and shelter you from Satan's evil schemes (See Psalm 91). Ask Jesus to help you trust Him in whatever difficulty you are facing. Watch how He sets you free from the cage of your fears ... forever.

A Good Report

The disciples returned to Jesus to give a report after casting out demons and healing the sick. Their testimonies brought glory to God and encouraged people around them too. People had tangible proof that God was working, and nothing was too difficult for Him.

As you think about the goodness of God and write down what He is doing in your life, you will give good reports also. Like the disciples, you will hear Jesus say in your heart, "I was watching Satan fall from heaven like lightning" (*Luke 10:18 NASB*) as your fears fall powerless before you.

God can do more in five minutes than we can in five hundred years. Reflecting on His love and grace places our hearts in the right place to partner with Him for His glory. Slowing down and taking time to revel in God's majesty simplifies our lives. It focuses us and makes us vessels of His power, just like the disciples were.

Sounds great, doesn't it? The only problem is Satan knows the OBSERVE Step strengthens us for battle too.

So the hater tries to distract you. He will do anything to stop you from looking to Jesus and remembering His goodness in your life. Instead of doing things in moderation, we binge. Binge eating. Binge television. Binge shopping. Binge sports.

Binging is irresponsible behavior—a way of escape. We binge to fill the love hole in our hearts. And it doesn't work.

Contemplation teaches you to binge on the love of God. And God's love works every time.

Some might say that taking time for thoughtful reflection is being irresponsible—a sign of laziness.

But taking the time to see God's goodness and acknowledging your fears through the eyes of Jesus leads to more action, not less. As God's love fills your life, you will want to change this broken world. Love is a verb. And that means action.

Want to have some fun? Do an act of kindness today and note which fear in your heart withers. Listen to it whine and say you don't love it anymore. Watch it plead for more attention. It will slowly starve to death as you give love to people and don't feed it any of your emotional energy.

That's right. The OBSERVE Step helps you improve your self-care. Bad experiences contribute to our fears, but we are the ones who decide to feed them or not. Fears can't survive unless we give them the energy to do so.

So, do what the disciples did. Give Jesus a report of the progress you are making and the problems you are facing. Talk to Jesus and explain how you are feeling and what you are thinking about your fears. Notice the following areas specifically and share the specifics with Jesus:

- Physically
- Mentally
- Emotionally
- Spiritually

Look into His loving eyes and give Jesus a full report. Hold nothing back. Tell Him everything. The longer your report, the less time your fears can multiply.

When you feel you are too tired to fight your fears, give Him a report.

When you don't know how to fight your fears, give Him a report.

Even when your fears seem so real you could touch them, give Him a report.

Then, ask Jesus what He sees and recommends you do about the fears. God loves when His children ask Him for wisdom. Too many believers depend on the world's wisdom, which clearly doesn't work very well against fear. Been there; done that.

When we ask for God's wisdom, the Bible says He pours it on us to overflowing. When we live our lives according to God's wisdom, we walk on the Path of Love. But you must ask.

> If any of you lacks wisdom, let him ask God, who gives generously to all without reproach, and it will be given him.
>
> James 1:5 (ESV)

God will cause the snow in the blizzard of your mind to fall to the ground. Your life's landscape becomes quiet, clear, and beautiful as far as the eye can see.

Calming The Storm

I love Rembrandt's painting *The Storm on the Sea of Galilee*. The waves crash, and the sky is dark. Some disciples work feverishly to regain control of the boat. Other disciples are gazing at Jesus. Some have perplexed faces. Others sit transfixed by the Prince of Peace.

Same event. Different interpretations of what was happening.

We have two choices about the fear in our lives. Some believers look at a negative experience and try to control its outcome. They are confused and wonder why God isn't answering their prayer. They fritter their spiritual lives away, trying to gain wealth, fame, and relationships to regain control and feel secure.

Other believers look to Jesus when something bad occurs in their life. They are transfixed by His love and power and believe He will act. They focus on the eternal, and God takes care of their earthly needs. They know fear is temporary.

There won't be any fear in heaven. Satan failed the entrance exam.

When Jesus faced the fierce storm, He said, "Peace, be still." And the storm stopped.

As you gaze at Jesus, you will see Him saying the same words to your fears. He doesn't put up with Satan. He doesn't have to. And neither do you.

I imagine the disciples had great confidence after they saw Jesus still the storm. They weren't too concerned the next time a storm battered their boat. When Jesus is in the boat, it's not going down.

Jesus has all authority, friend. So, you aren't going down either.

> *Peace I leave with you; my peace I give to you. Not as the world gives do I give to you. Let not your hearts be troubled, neither let them be afraid.*
>
> *John 14:27 (ESV)*

Reflect on the greatness of God when your fears roar and scream for attention. Remember the Father is above you. The Holy Spirit is in you. And Jesus is with you, carrying you like a lamb on His shoulders. He strokes your tangled wool, softly singing, "It is Well with My Soul."

▼ ▼ ▼ ▼ ▼

You have been given so many talents and spiritual resources to fight your fears. But the hurricane of fear keeps you from seeing them. The OBSERVE Step helps you rediscover them.

Let today be the day you pick them up and use all your gifts for God's glory. Leo Buscaglia said it best, "Your talent is God's gift to you. What you do with it is your gift back to God."

Observing your fears slows them down and allows God to replace them with His love. We will look at how He does that in the next chapter.

Questions for Reflection

1. In what ways do you feel God is working on your fears since you started reading this book?

2. How do you see Jesus in the details of your day-to-day life?

3. Describe a time when you felt God's love in a huge situation or problem?

4. List five specific ways you can show kindness to others. Now, write down how it makes you feel thinking about the kind things you can do for these people.

5. Reflect on God's goodness in your life. Spend some extra time thanking Him today.

7

HIS LOVE SURROUNDS ME

*We ourselves feel that what we are doing is just
a drop in the ocean. But the ocean would be less
because of that missing drop.*

- MOTHER TERESA

You have identified the voice speaking the fear. Then, you observed how the fear is hurting your mind, heart, body, and soul through the eyes of Jesus.

Now it's time to fill your tank with God's never-ending love. The VALUE Step of the LOVE Plan helps you feel the same about yourself that God feels about you.

Before we go any further, though, I must admit I'm a little concerned at this point.

Why?

Because Satan may or may not fight your efforts to apply the first and second steps of the LOVE Plan. But when you live out step three, the hater will step up the attack for sure.

He will parade negative thoughts across your mind. He will tell you the LOVE Plan doesn't work. He'll convince you it's not all that bad to have fears.

The enemy will engineer bad experiences to discourage you. The Fake Fears channel will run continuously in your mind and heart. Satan will do anything to stop you from loving yourself the way God loves you.

And if all that doesn't work, the imposter will remind you of good experiences in your past. Fun times with friends and family, only to jog your memory about how it all ended badly and how your future will be filled with disappointments.

That's why the biblical truths in this chapter are so important. You have listened to the Good Shepherd. You have observed how He responds to your fear. Now you absolutely must cling to His everlasting love.

You must value yourself the same way He does.

Love Wins

Experiencing God's love gives you the reserves you need to crush your fears. Perfect love casts out fear (*1 John 4:18, NASB*).

Satan will tempt you to slip back into fears with negative thoughts. He will try to convince you that you are powerless to change. He will point out all the times you failed on the battlefield with him. Satan wants your past failures and losses to dictate your present and future outcomes.

The hater fills your life with fears and scammers on the radio, television, and computer screen. He wants you to worry about everything going on in the world. He wants you to take the bait of believing you must care for yourself and everyone else because you don't have a Good Shepherd who's taking care of you.

And just when you have conquered one fear, the accuser will send seven more. He wants to overwhelm you with false positives and discourage you from even trying to stop your negative thinking.

Let's be honest. You are reading this book because you want to help someone you care about to overcome their fears. They are trying to stop the fears that crowd their thoughts. But fears are affecting their life in increasingly bad ways.

Maybe it's a friend, a spouse, a child, or perhaps it's you.

You had a plan. You worked the plan. But it didn't work. And Satan hisses, "No plan will ever work for you. You'll never overcome your fears."

The Father of Lies strikes again.

We live in a broken world, and love can be hard to find at times. Every person is facing their own internal battles. This means even people who love us can't always give us the love we need. Many of us haven't experienced much real love in our lives, and for that reason, we struggle with fear.

Add the bad experiences of guilt trips, being left out of the group, standing alone as the last one picked on the playground, and people being fast to criticize and slow to praise—it's a jungle out there!

You may not remember the last time your love tank was full. Or even half full.

The lack of love in our lives breeds fears, which in turn disturb everything we do. Instead of a soft answer, we give a harsh one. Instead of cooperating, we compete with our friends. Instead of having self-confidence, we shrink back from the tasks God has asked us to do.

But God has promised you inner peace and security. That is the divine LOVE Plan for you. God's heart is to fill your love tank to overflowing every day, so fear doesn't stand a chance.

> *No, despite all these things, overwhelming victory is ours through Christ, who loved us.*
>
> Romans 8:37 (NLT)

That's why the LOVE Plan is so important. It shows you how to fill your love tank and replace the cancerous fears plaguing you with God's love.

Being Present

Ever notice how you can spend more time thinking about bad events in the past than the good things God has done? This is a sure sign you are walking on the Path of Fear.

Satan tempts you to fall for fears that have made you worry in the past. The LOVE Plan puts you back on the Love Path and brings the focus back to the present.

The key to returning to the Path of Love is valuing yourself like Jesus values you. God valued you so much that He gave His only Son to die for you—to take your punishment—so you could have an intimate relationship with your Creator. And that's just the beginning of how God has shown His love for you. Open your heart and mind to all the ways God loves you right now.

Jesus is always with you. He is always present. That's because love is ... being fully present.

Jesus left heaven and came to earth, so He could be present with us. He showed us how to be present with God, present with others, and present with ourselves.

After Jesus returned to heaven, He sent the Holy Spirit to be present in us. Helping us love God, others, and ourselves.

I will ask the Father, and He will give you another Helper, that He may be with you forever; that is the Spirit of truth, whom the world cannot receive, because it does not see Him or know Him, but you know Him because He abides with you and will be in you.

John 14:16–17 (NASB)

God's love is always present.

That's how I know you can go through life with a full love tank. It is possible. What's impossible with us, is possible for the Lover of our souls.

By the way, this is an excellent way to evaluate any plan to overcome fear.

Does it help you be more present?

Present for the ones you love. Present for God. Present for yourself.

Satan gasps in panic when he sees you living in the present rather than stuck in the past or worried about the future.

Satan wants you to get so caught up in fake fears that you aren't ready to deal with real fears when they come. When you spend so much emotional and physical energy combating fears crying wolf, you cannot rise above a real crisis when it comes.

You are too worn down to be present. That is fear's knock-out punch.

The hater will use your failure in a real crisis as ammunition to keep you in the past. He wants you to keep mulling over what went wrong and beat yourself up about it. Satan works hard to keep you stuck in the past.

Satan enjoys convincing you to beat yourself up, so he doesn't have to. He's evil like that.

The tempter wants you to overthink everything. He wants you to be consumed with your guilt, not God's forgiveness. Satan wants you to feel rejected, not accepted; shame, not honor, and blame, not approval.

But the LOVE Plan puts you squarely in the present. And that's where Jesus is. Always present. Always loving you.

Good News

Satan hates it when you meditate on how much God loves you. He squirms when he sees you basking in the glow of knowing your heavenly Father is your biggest fan. It reminds your enemy that he has lost the fight against God.

Love has won. Hate has lost.

> *"For I know the plans I have for you"—this is the LORD's declaration—"plans for your welfare, not for disaster, to give you a future and a hope."*
>
> *Jeremiah 29:11 (HCSB)*

Nevertheless, Satan does his best to distract you from God's goodness and blessings in your life. He knows if he can get you focused on your problems, it will open up a foothold to fear. Fears swirl in your mind:

- Do my friends care about me, or are they just pretending to care?
- Will my children contract an incurable disease?
- Will my parents need care in their later years that I won't be able to provide?
- Is my company going to survive these turbulent economic times?

Satan convinces you the future will always be bad. You will have fears every day for the rest of your life. And they will grow bigger and turn more sinister.

Satan laughs, saying, "You haven't seen anything yet, pathetic one."

And it's hard not to believe the deceiver. Circumstances are getting worse for some people in our world.

There are more economic problems, environmental problems, political problems, and social problems.

Increasing school shootings ... rising rape cases ... escalating emotional abuse ... climbing credit card debt.

Of course, you should take commonsense approaches to protect yourself, but most of this news is a false alarm... for you. Real fears for others.

But not real for you.

And worrying about everyone else's problems empties your love tank and limits your ability to deal with your problems.

Write this on a sticky note and put it on your refrigerator door: "Most fears are false alarms and drain my love tank."

But you might say, "I need to know about the world around me."

Or, "I watch the news because I care about others and want to pray for them."

Or, "I worry about others because I love them so much."

Sounds great. But these are excuses to justify worry and fear in your life. It's important to be informed, pray, and love others. Satan, however, is using your good intentions to tempt you to fear, just like he did with Eve in the garden.

He knows the more time you spend watching the news, the more fears you will struggle with. What a mess.

When Satan tries his old tricks in your life again, you have a simple way to defeat him.

You have the third step of the LOVE Plan:

You decide to value yourself the way God values you. This is Satan's greatest fear—that you would understand how valuable you are to God. When you truly see and value yourself the way God does, fear can't grip you or torment you any longer. Satan is powerless to torture or defeat you with guilt, rejection, shame, or blame.

As you understand your value to God more and more, all kinds of good things happen. You make decisions based on love and not fear—the way of wisdom. Loving yourself more gives you the capacity to love others better.

You look forward to the new ways you will experience God's love today and tomorrow. Your heart and mind work together to give everything you do meaning and purpose.

Perhaps you struggle with valuing yourself. Maybe you don't know what valuing yourself in a healthy way looks like, especially if you have experienced cruel treatment by people who valued themselves in unhealthy ways. "I don't want to be like that," you say. I don't blame you; neither do I.

Maybe adults pushed you down emotionally as a child. Now you feel like everyone in the crowd is valuable, except you. You know it isn't true in your head, but your heart says differently.

The good news is God's Holy Spirit lives in you and is transforming you. And the biggest change we can ever make is knowing how much God cherishes us.

Spend time every day meditating on how much God values you. Ask Him to help you see yourself the way He sees you. Remember all the blessings in your life, past and present. Watch your fears melt away and return to the waterless places where they belong as you feel how valuable you are to your Father.

Love conquers all. Perfect love casts out fear. God so loved that He gave. God's love is forever. And He's transforming you into something beautiful.

Something Beautiful

Satan will try to convince us to put on our detective hats and find all the bad in this world. When God created the world, He said, "It is good." Satan doesn't want us to believe this truth.

But people are doing so many beautiful and life-giving acts in the world right now. God is at work. His kingdom is coming. Satan's forces have been defeated, and we are in the clean-up campaign. We just have to look around and see what He has done and is doing.

These years of struggle will be like a few seconds once we get to heaven. Earnest believers sometimes live as if Satan is winning the battle, though. They believe this world will end badly. They believe Satan's smoke and mirrors performance.

But if we'll stop and listen, the Spirit is restless in our hearts saying, "It's not true. God has this. God has you."

> *For God has not given us a Spirit of fearfulness, but one of power, love, and sound judgment.*
>
> *2 Timothy 1:7 (HCSB)*

The Spirit surges with power within us and wants to make the world a better place. He gives strength, hope, and confidence.

But when we believe the fear fibsters, we feel like we can't make a difference. We feel powerless to change the world. We feel powerless to change ourselves. We wonder if we will ever be free.

And this grieves the Spirit of God because it's just not true:

- God has promised we can hear His voice.
- God has promised to care for us like a Good Shepherd.
- God has promised nothing can separate us from His love.
- God has promised the Spirit as a down payment of future glory.

God has this, friend. And He's got you.

Good-bye, fears.

Hello, faith, hope, and love.

In the next chapter, you will learn four ways to take your faith to a new level using the EXPECT Step.

Questions for Reflection

1. How have you learned to value yourself as God values you?

2. In what ways do you feel better equipped to crush your fears?

3. How will you fill your love tank?

4. How is the Holy Spirit transforming you?

5. Do an internet search to find five examples of people doing kind things for one another in our ugly world. How are you encouraged by this?

8

HE IS ALWAYS WITH ME

You don't have to see the whole staircase, just take the first step.

- MARTIN LUTHER KING, JR.

Struggling with fears sure can feel lonely. Many people don't understand how real fears can feel, like a dark, menacing cloud threatening to pour down on you. Even friends tell you just to buck up and stop being such a worrywart. They mean well; they just don't understand.

But God understands. That's why He sent the Holy Spirit to lead us into the truth. We are not alone when we face our fears. We always have a Partner. And our Partner has been around longer than Satan.

Fears come from many places and times in our lives. Fighting them can be like playing the "pound the prairie dog's head with the hammer" game. As soon as you deal with one, two more pop up.

If you had an emotionally abusive childhood as I did, fears take root in your life at an early age. Maybe they grew in your life for many years before you recognized them. But now you know how harmful they are to your soul, and you're working on destroying their power in your life.

The fourth step of the Love Plan is EXPECT. You expect Jesus to be with you in every circumstance and help you get to the other side. The Bible calls this kind of belief ... faith.

You might wonder how our family trained 5,000 believers overseas to follow Jesus in Buddhist countries and how we were able to see 1,200 discipleship groups and 300 churches start. I can tell you in one word—expect.

In this chapter, you will learn some practical tips to make the EXPECT Step your own.

Many people believe they must make big changes in their life to defeat their fears. Although that may be true sometimes, that simply isn't true many times. Each step of the Love Plan is simple and small. Their power comes from doing them repeatedly and making them a consistent part of your life—every single day.

For example, if I asked you to shoot ten free-throw shots on a basketball court, what would your shooting percentage be? 50 percent? 80 percent? 8 percent?

But what if you attempted 400 free-throw shots almost every day for the next ten years of your life? What would your percentage be then? How would it improve your game? Ask Michael Jordan. That was his routine.

If you did that many free-throw shots every day, you would expect you would make most of them. And the same is true for all the steps in the Love Plan. The more you do them, the more you will expect to conquer any fear that comes your way.

So, let's start shooting!

Take a Selfie

Have you ever noticed Jesus isn't present in your fears? If you look around the fearful picture in your mind, He isn't anywhere, is He? What gives?

When the dark voices in your head paint fears, they must leave Jesus out. Jesus has conquered fear, and His presence ruins their evil schemes. Your fears aren't as big when Jesus is in the house. In fact, they bow to Jesus!

So, step four of the LOVE Plan is to EXPECT Jesus to be with you. All the time. Everywhere.

> *"And surely I am with you always, to the very end of the age."*
>
> *Matthew 28:20 (NIV)*

I want you to try something that has worked well for me. The next time fear overwhelms you, take a selfie with Jesus in the bad circumstance. Feeling bold? Ask the ferocious fear if you can take a selfie with it and Jesus. Really makes the devil's head spin. He doesn't like it at all.

Jesus smiles because He knows He has defeated them all.

Jesus promised He would always be with us. And the Word of God is forever true. Even in our fears, Jesus is with us, if we let Him.

Jesus was there when you were born and on your first day of school. He was with you when you left home, and He is with you now. He will be with you tomorrow, and He will be there when you take your last breath.

He is the Great I Am.

You can expect Jesus to show you the best path for your life because He promised He would. You can expect Jesus to cleanse and heal you from every sin because He gave His word that He would.

You can expect to become more like Jesus every day. You can expect every day to be full of His presence no matter what you are facing.

And when you have no idea where to turn, expect Jesus to walk beside you with confidence and comfort. He knows you better than you know yourself. He will provide.

The world is full of real danger. Let's not kid ourselves. Bullies, cheaters, scam artists, and warmongers are for real. Acting like they don't exist only empowers them more and feeds the fear in your life.

Instead of focusing on the evil in the world and the negativity that surrounds us, God's Word instructs us to think about good, positive things:

> *And now, dear brothers and sisters, one final thing. Fix your thought on what is true, and honorable, and right, and pure, and lovely, and admirable. Think about things that are excellent and worthy of praise.*
>
> *Philippians 4:8 (NLT)*

By the way, selfies with Jesus are the best! Why? Because Jesus brings His peace and love into the picture while driving out Satan and fear.

Change the Channel

Expecting Jesus to be with you gives you the ability to analyze events around you accurately. Beware of Satan's schemes; he likes to use fear to overwhelm your mind, so you can't discern his lies, and you wind up blindly following him on the Path of Fear.

Remember—God has given you the Holy Spirit to judge truth, but Satan uses fear to short-circuit your ability to see clearly.

Satan works hard at convincing you to view the present with skepticism. He wants you to feel insecure around people and worry about your money, your job, your health, and your children.

The hater will do anything to discourage you, cloud your mind, and snooker you into bad decisions. If he can make your picture of the future look gray, instead of colorful, he roars in victory.

The LOVE Plan, however, gives you solid biblical steps to overcome the enemy's tactics. Follow the plan, and you crush fear the same way Jesus did when He walked on the earth.

You will hear the voice of your Good Shepherd, sense His care, be filled with His love, and know He is always with you. His perfect love will cast out your fears.

> *There is no fear in love, but perfect love casts out fear. For fear has to do with punishment, and whoever fears has not been perfected in love.*
>
> *1 John 4:18 (ESV)*

Seems like following the plan of the Creator of this world is a smart course to take. I'll take His plan over mine any day of the week!

The fourth step of the LOVE Plan will bless you in many ways. Expecting Jesus to be with you will:

- Help you be positive in the now
- Make you feel secure
- Inspire you to make good decisions
- Create optimism for the future

The fourth step of the LOVE Plan helps you change the channel you have been watching in your mind. The new channel always has Jesus. The old channel usually didn't.

The new channel has worship and praise. The old channel had worry and paranoia.

The new channel creates trust and confidence. The old channel caused terror and confusion.

The call letters of the new channel are faith, hope, and love. The call letters of the old channel were unbelief, despair, and hate.

The new channel is playing in heaven. The old channel is playing in hell.

Which channel are you watching?

A New Language

Ever notice how the same fears keep showing up repeatedly? They are like cockroaches in the kitchen—just when you think they are gone, you see another one.

And if you don't have heavy boots on, what's a person to do?

When we don't take responsibility for fighting our fears, we allow them to give birth to new fears in dark places. That's why the LOVE Plan is so important. Now you have a biblical plan that allows you to take control of your life rather than be infested with fears.

Expecting Jesus to be with you in the EXPECT Step not only changes the way you think but also changes the way you talk to yourself.

Imagine this: you're sitting on a bench in a park, and Jesus is sitting beside you. Would you think or say things like ...?

- I'm such a loser. I can't defeat my fears.
- I'm such a nobody. I can't be loved.
- I'm such a freak. I just want to disappear.
- I'm such a mess up. I can't do anything right.

Truly, truly, I say to you, Jesus would be heartbroken to hear His masterpiece being criticized so unfairly. He would know Satan had tricked you into walking the Path of Fear.

Jesus wants you to learn a new language. Can you imagine Jesus saying the statements above? No way! The Holy Spirit inside you will teach you how to talk to yourself like Jesus talked to Himself.

In the power of the Spirit, Jesus spoke truth, loved deeply, healed the sick, and overcame the enemy. And because Jesus sent you His Spirit, that is your destiny as well.

Knowing Jesus is always with you increases your self-confidence. More is caught than taught, friend. Just being close to Jesus's supreme confidence will give you greater confidence too.

Expect Jesus to be the same today as He was when He walked the dusty roads of Galilee. Expect Him always to be present. Notice how confident He is. Feel His strength in your heart. Copy who He is and what He does.

> *Imitate God, therefore, in everything you do, because you are his dear children. Live a life filled with love, following the example of Christ. He loved us and offered himself as a sacrifice for us, a pleasing aroma to God.*
>
> *Ephesians 5:1–2 (NLT)*

Expect the Good Shepherd to walk beside you and stop every fear. Talk to Him. LISTEN to how He talks to you. Copy what He says.

Then you will understand why God allowed fear to remain in this world—to force us to depend on Him instead of ourselves.

The key to overcoming fear lies in what you expect. If you expect the worst, your fears will multiply. If you expect the best, Jesus will give you the shield of faith against every foe.

The Spirit gives you the power to keep going, even when your heart hurts, reminding you there is a victor's crown for every fight. And the last time I checked, the Spirit is always right.

This expectation—this faith—makes you more and more like Jesus. I can't think of anything better. Can you?

Even when tough times come—and we both know they will—God is working. Someday God will reward you in heaven according to how you handled your fears.

Practicing the EXPECT Step opens your heart to the Holy Spirit of God in faith. He takes your faith, adds hope, and fills you with His love.

Then, you begin to speak a new language—words of fear are long gone—now you're speaking the language of love. And people know us by the words we speak.

The Father's Love

Did you know your relationship with others is often an indicator of your relationship with God? For example, how you treat others usually reflects the way you believe God treats you.

If you are critical, demanding, and rude—that's probably how you think God views you. And that's a scary world to live in. If you are caring, helpful, and kind, that's an outward demonstration of what you think in your heart about how God treats you.

This leads to the next question: Are your fears hurting your connections with family and friends? Are you critical, demanding, and rude? Or caring, helpful, and gracious? If so, that could be a sign that you need to crush some fears in your life and be filled with more of God's love. It's time to put the LOVE Plan into full gear!

When you have relationship struggles, you can handle them with God's wisdom. The Holy Spirit will help you when you listen, observe, value, and expect like Jesus.

And the good news is, as you become more like Jesus, others in your family will too. Each person is responsible for their spiritual journey with Jesus. It certainly doesn't hurt to have a good example to follow, though. The LOVE Plan helps you be an excellent example.

Be imitators of me, as I am of Christ.

1 Corinthians 11:1 (ESV)

Imagine for a moment what your family will be like when everyone runs with full love tanks. Picture what your friendships will be like when everyone doubles their love and halves their fears.

Sounds like heaven to me. No more fears. No more tears. Just love, as far as the eye can see. This is God's kingdom come on earth as it is in heaven!

Expecting to see Jesus exercises your faith and shows you He was there all the time. Fears had blinded your eyes to His presence. Now you know how deep the Father's love is for you, and you know how close He is … always.

Armed with the Father's love, Satan's pathetic attempts to create fear in your heart and mind will be obvious. Instead of doubting God's love, you will doubt Satan's schemes.

Use the LOVE Plan every day, and you will reach the point where you laugh at Satan's bewilderment as he flees from you, unable to terrorize you with his fear. God's love will surround you and foil the hater's hatred.

God made our hearts to grow in love. Having children doesn't cause our love to divide but multiply. In the same way, knowing how deep the Father's love is for you can multiply through every relationship you hold dear.

What a wonderful gift to give children: how to listen to God, to know His eye watches over them, to feel God say, "You are my beloved," and to grow their faith by expecting Jesus to be with them always.

Follow the LOVE Plan, and very soon, you will see results in your family that you could never have dreamed. Even in the darkest times, you will see a light shining. When you find your heart burdened, you will feel God filling you with His love.

Even so, Lord Jesus, come quickly.

Questions for Reflection

1. In what ways have you been surprised that Jesus is with you in all circumstances?
2. How does it comfort you knowing Jesus is in the selfie with you?
3. How will you change the channels when fear comes at you?
4. Write down three positive things about yourself.
5. What changes will you make to respond to your family lovingly?

CONCLUSION

I prayed to the lord, and he answered me. He
freed me from all my fears.

- PSALM 34:4 (NLT)

We live in a world full of terror. Atomic bombs. Jihads. Sociopaths. Pedophiles. Global warming. Economic recessions.

Many people constantly worry about tomorrow. They feel like their best days are behind them, and the future will get worse and worse. They act in fearful, suspicious ways.

It seems like many of us have become emotional zombies.

I heard somewhere that the average fifth grader has the same stress level today that an adult had seventy years ago. Not sure if that's true. But it sure seems like it could be, and it explains the large numbers of children who deal with anxiety daily. Many of us just don't feel safe anymore.

If we're not careful, this environment can convince us that negative thinking is okay. But it's not. God isn't wringing His hands in heaven, and neither should we on earth.

Most fears we feel are ... cheaters and con men.

Satan tempted Eve with the supernatural ability to tell good from evil. Today, the news media tempts us with the supernatural ability to know all the good and bad throughout the world. Satan's masterful trick?

Sounds like a bad sequel to the Garden of Eden. (Could someone throw a truckload of rotten tomatoes, please?)

Ninety-five percent of what we watch is bad news. And that's not good.

Satan has a vested interest in causing you to be suspicious and skeptical of God's love. The more the hater carries out his devious plan, the more he chains you on the Path of Fear.

Millions of believers today are bound by fear, anxiety, and worry, and as a result, they cannot grow to be more like Jesus.

Fears come from unhealthy thinking, and the Bible says to take our thoughts captive to the truth. But how?

Some say that you can "out-think" your fears. Quote enough Bible verses, and they will go away. Learn enough about God's Word, and fears will vanish. "Just trust God," they say.

Both Scripture memory and Bible study help but are only part of the solution. Why? Because fear is both a head and a heart problem.

Satan has engineered traumatic events in your past that planted the seeds of guilt, rejection, shame, and blame in your heart. And the Bible says, "As a man thinks in his heart, so is he" (Proverbs 23:7 ESV).

I have seen how fears can wound the soul, especially after losing my wife to cancer. Believing the lies of smoke-and-mirror fears drained my self-confidence, and I walked the Path of Fear for many months.

Then, the Spirit of God reminded me of the truths He had taught me about fear—lessons I had taught others.

He held me close even while I struggled to escape His love because of my hurt. He cleaned my wounds, and I cried. He took my hand in His and gently brought me back onto the Path of Love. Praise His name.

I wrote this book because I want that for you, dear child of God.

The LOVE Plan gives you a way to imitate Jesus when you are fighting your fears. Jesus listened to His Father. At His baptism, Jesus knew His Father was observing Him when He heard, "This is my beloved Son, with whom I am well pleased" (Matthew 3:17 ESV). He knew His Father valued Him and would always be there for Him.

The LOVE Plan is simply facing fear the way Jesus faced fear.

He won. He lives in you. You can win too.

The LOVE Plan is based on the Truth, not Satan's smooth fear operators. The LOVE Plan is based on faithful love, not fearful death.

As you apply this plan to your life, you will walk in truth, and your confidence in God will grow. And greater confidence in God always leads to greater self-confidence.

You will discover inner peace as you love others. You will experience serenity as you learn how to love yourself better.

You will smell the stench of Satan's lies a mile away. He will no longer be your deceiver but the defeated one. You will know fake fears are a sign to refill your love tank.

What Satan tries to do for evil, you will turn to good.

Even when you face new fears, you will have a plan that defeats any fear: past, present, or future. You won't wonder what to do when the fiery missiles of fear burst around your heart and mind.

And at the end of your life, you will realize your fears actually drew you closer to God. You'll find your ability to hear His voice and look into His eyes grew with every fear you defeated. Jesus will feel closer than you could ever have imagined.

The road will rise to meet you. Your heart will be strangely warmed by the love of Jesus as you walk with Him in the cool of the day. And you will look back over your life knowing for certain ... fear was a liar.

Questions for Reflection

1. Describe how your thinking has changed about fear and God's love for you.
2. How will you continue to change your thinking?
3. In what ways has your confidence in God grown?
4. How have you drawn closer to God through this study?
5. What specific things will you do to respond differently the next time hurts or fears come into your life?

CAN YOU HELP?

Before you go, I'd like to say "thank you" again for buying this guide on how to defeat fear and feel the love of God again. I know you could have picked from dozens of books, but you chose this one. So, a big thanks for downloading this book and reading it all the way to the end.

Now I'd like to ask for a *small* favor. Could you please take a minute or two and leave a short review for this book at http://go.lightkeeperbooks.com/e-fil-rev? There is no greater way to thank me than this!

Think of it as a testimony to other believers about how this book helped you and could benefit them.

And if you loved it, then please let me know that too!

BONUS

Don't forget to download your free *Powerful Prayers Bonus Pak*! The free Pak includes three resources to help you pray powerful prayers:

- 100 Promises – Audio Version
- 40 Faith-Building Quotes
- 40 Powerful Prayers.

All are suitable for framing. Download your free *Powerful Prayers Bonus Pak* at go.lightkeeperbooks.com/powerpak

I've also included an excerpt from my bestselling book *Fear is a Liar*. God has blessed many through this book and I wanted to give you a chance to "try before you buy." To order *Fear is a Liar*, visit go.lightkeeperbooks.com/e-fil

POWERFUL
PRAYERS
— IN THE —
WAR ROOM

DANIEL B LANCASTER PhD

INTRODUCTION

The one concern of the devil is to keep Christians from praying. He fears nothing from prayerless studies, prayerless work and prayerless religion. He laughs at our toil, mocks at our wisdom, but he trembles when we pray.

- SAMUEL CHADWICK

This is a simple book on prayer.

You will learn the most important lessons I've gathered about prayer in the last 40 years – principles I wish people had taught me long ago. I'm not as powerful a prayer warrior as I want to be, but the truths I will share with you have helped my prayer life a great deal. The lessons you will learn in this book have helped me, and I believe will help you, too.

For many years, prayer was frustrating and hard for me to do consistently. This was my problem: I wanted to pray, I had been told I should pray, but I didn't know how to pray. When I tried to pray my mind would wander, I found myself bored, and I felt prayer was a complicated exercise I could never master. Just being honest. Conversations with other believers convinced me I wasn't the only one feeling that way about prayer. Earnest followers of Jesus shared similar thoughts.

When our family of six moved to Southeast Asia as missionaries, spiritual warfare became a real issue. Having pastored in America, my prayer life had looked like a roller coaster – some highs, but mostly lows, twists, and turns. Working with national believers for twelve years overseas, I was struck with how they prayed powerful prayers and I didn't. I don't mean emotional prayers; I mean prayers that were answered in ways that brought glory to God and saw His kingdom advance on the earth.

So, I started a journey of learning how to pray. Although I read many books on prayer, my main strategy was to look in the Bible and see how Jesus prayed and what He prayed about during his ministry. Then, I tried to copy Him in a way that would forge a habit. The rest of the book outlines the helpful gems I learned: the four weapons of prayer, seven powerful prayer topics, four ways God answers prayer, three war room prayer strategies, and nine tips to improve your prayer life.

We need powerful prayer warriors in the war room if our world is going to change. Clearly, most of the problems the church faces today are from a lack of prayer. Use this book to learn how to pray better. Use it to teach your children and grandchildren. God has always used the simple things to confound the wise. My prayer is God would use me and you to change the world one more time. Change, I believe, will only come on our knees.

1

FOUR WEAPONS OF POWERFUL PRAYER

When the devil sees a man or woman who really believes in prayer, who knows how to pray, and who really does pray, and, above all, when he sees a whole church on its face before god in prayer, he trembles as much as he ever did, for he knows that his day in that church or community is at an end.

- R.A. TORREY

Many people struggle with knowing how to pray. I know I have through the years. They have heard many times they should pray, but never received the tools to do so. They enter the War Room of prayer empty-handed and soon grow discouraged. They find themselves wishing they could pray better and feeling guilty they don't.

As you enter the War Room, remember Jesus is with you. He is the Great High Priest and knows how to pray perfectly. During his ministry on earth, Jesus showed his disciples how to pray, and he wants to show you how to pray too. Few actions make Jesus happier than when one of his children bow beside him and join him in prayer!

In this section, you will learn four weapons of powerful prayer: praise, repentance, asking, and yielding. Each part is important to a healthy prayer life. If your prayer life is dry or boring, usually the reason is one of the four weapons of prayer is missing. Make each weapon of powerful prayer a habit and watch your prayer life grow.

Praise

The right way to pray is to stretch out our hands and ask of one who we know has the heart of a father.

– DIETRICH BONHOEFFER

Praise is the first weapon in powerful prayer. Each of Jesus's recorded prayers starts with praise and we should copy Him. Luke 10:21 says:

At that very time He rejoiced greatly in the Holy Spirit, and said, "I praise You, O Father, Lord of heaven and earth, that You have hidden these things from the wise and intelligent and have revealed them to infants. Yes, Father, for this way was well-pleasing in Your sight."

(Matthew 11:25 NASB)

It makes sense for praise to be the first part of prayer. When we begin to pray, we are ushered into the throne room of Almighty God – with the angels and seraphim. Other believers join us before God's throne. Throughout the Bible, the first response people make in God's presence is worship.

Why is praise a powerful weapon when we pray?

We were created to love God and people, but because of original sin, we found ourselves in circumstances where we hurt others, and others hurt us. Soon we developed the idea our main task was to guard our heart. We built walls to keep others out. Occasionally, we would let someone in, but doing so terrified us, and we soon found a reason to kick them out.

The result is we have small hearts. In fact, as time passed our hearts grew smaller and smaller.

Praise is an important weapon in the war room of prayer because it makes our hearts bigger – we understand who God is and what He can do

Praise opens our heart to God. Praise connects us with the Everlasting Father. Praise pulls us out of our little world and gives us the bigger picture of God's sovereign kingdom.

When I start my prayer with praise, it sounds something like this:

> *Heavenly Father. I praise you. You are good. You are strong. You are our deliverer. You are the Everlasting One. You set a table before us. You lead us to green pastors. There is none like you. Awesome in all your deeds. Your hand is not too short to save. You have loved us with an everlasting love.*

This is an example of a prayer of praise. Practice praising God in prayer until you feel your heart is bigger and you see God in His splendor. I use this hand motion to remind myself which part of prayer I am doing.

After you spend time praising God, move to the next weapon of powerful prayer: repentance.

Repent

If you find your life of prayer to be always so short, and so easy, and so spiritual, as to be without cost and strain and sweat to you, you may depend upon it, you have not yet begun to pray.

– ALEXANDER WHYTE

The second weapon of powerful prayer is repentance. I've noticed when I praise God with all my heart, I become more aware of my sin. When I see holy God, I also see my faults.

Feelings of inadequacy, fears, struggles, and other difficulties rise from my heart. In fact, I question whether I am praising God with all of my heart if this doesn't happen!

How do you deal with those negative thoughts and feelings? Jesus shared a parable about two different ways people deal with their sin in Luke 18:9-14:

> *Jesus told a story to some people who thought they were better than others and who looked down on everyone else:*

> *Two men went into the temple to pray. One was a Pharisee and the other a tax collector. The Pharisee stood over by himself and prayed, "God, I thank you that I am not greedy, dishonest, and unfaithful in marriage like other people. And I am really glad that I am not like that tax collector over there. I go without eating for two days a week, and I give you one tenth of all I earn."*

> *The tax collector stood off at a distance and did not think he was good enough even to look up toward heaven. He was so sorry for what he had done that he pounded his chest and prayed, "God, have pity on me! I am such a sinner."*

> *Then Jesus said, "When the two men went home, it was the tax collector and not the Pharisee who was pleasing to God. If you put yourself above others, you will be put down. But if you humble yourself, you will be honored."*

> *(CEV)*

Some people don't deal with their sin when they pray. Instead, they think about their good deeds and the bad deeds of others. Psychologists call this misdirection. The Pharisee in Jesus' parable hardened his heart by judging others. Throughout the Bible, God cautions He will not listen to a hard-hearted person.

People like the tax collector choose to repent of their sins – owning their faults. Repenting means to admit our sin openly, feel remorse, and turn away from committing it again. This is what the tax collector did, and Jesus said he went home justified – God had heard his prayer. Repenting pleases God and connects us with His heart when we pray.

People are uncomfortable with the idea we will all face a judgment day. We feel like we are barely keeping up with our lives as it is and rationalize that God will overlook our sin. We spurn judgment day because our hearts are stubborn. We don't want to admit our wrongdoing and come up with flimsy excuses to explain it away. Comparing ourselves with others is how we usually do this. We say, "I'm not like ISIS, or people who riot, or..."

When God brings up the truth of my sin, I have two choices: I can repent or I can harden my heart. Repentance is a powerful prayer weapon in the war room, because our hearts are hard and need to be soft towards God.

When I pray the "repent" part of my prayers, I talk to God saying:

> Lord, forgive me for my anger and how I treated my friend yesterday. I was thinking selfishly and pushing my agenda. I hurt her, and I am sorry. I could tell you were displeased and you have convicted me several times since then, but I haven't cared and have hardened my heart. Please forgive me and help me as I apologize to my friend today. Soften my heart towards you and her. I repent of my sin.

Your prayer will be different, but I wanted to provide an example. Here is the "repent" hand motion.

After spending time repenting of your sins and softening your heart before God, move to the third weapon of powerful prayer: asking.

This is an excerpt from Dr. Lancaster's bestselling book – Powerful Prayers in the War Room. You can download it from Amazon by clicking https://www.amazon.com/dp/B019R1ZOU8

MORE FROM THIS AUTHOR

#1 Best Sellers

on

amazon

This series on powerful prayer, heart-felt worship, and intimacy with Christ will help strengthen your "War Room" and give you a battle plan for prayer.

Visit go.lightkeeperbooks.com/battleplan
to learn more.

ABOUT THE AUTHOR

Daniel B. Lancaster (PhD) enjoys training others to become passionate followers of Christ. He has planted two churches in America and trained over 5,000 people in Southeast Asia as a strategy coordinator with the International Mission Board. He served as Assistant Vice-President for University Ministries at Union University and currently is the Director of Coaching at Cornerstone International. He has four grown children and a delightful grandson.

Dr. Dan is available for speaking and training events. Contact him at dan@lightkeeperbooks.com to arrange a meeting for your group.

Made in the USA
Coppell, TX
04 February 2023

12170757R00079